for Pat Carroll

Richard Hill

April 1983

The Royal Navy

Today and Tomorrow

Rear Admiral J.R.Hill

LONDON

IAN ALLAN LTD

Contents

First published 1981
Reprinted 1982

ISBN 0 7110 1168 0

© J. R. Hill, 1981

Published by Ian Allan Ltd, Shepperton, Surrey;
and printed by Ian Allan Printing Ltd at their works
at Coombelands in Runnymede, England

*The views expressed in this book are the
author's own and do not necessarily
represent the opinion or policy of Her
Majesty's Goverment.*

To my wife Patricia
Who supported it,
Read it, critically,
And typed it, even,
      this book is dedicated.

Foreword

by Admiral Sir Henry Leach, GCB, ADC, First Sea Lord

I am glad to have the opportunity to write this Foreword to *The Royal Navy Today and Tomorrow*. It is the first comprehensive and illustrated work of its kind for many years and will occupy an important place in our affairs.

It is now more than 40 years since the start of World War II. Half the people in our country are too young to remember it. Of the remainder too great a proportion find it more convenient, more comfortable and considerably cheaper to forget it. Over the years many have come to take the Royal Navy for granted; and the fact that a grey hull is often around where and when it is most needed is accepted as commonplace. Today *people* travel by air and are inclined to forget that *things* still have to go largely by sea.

This book is timely in reminding us of these things: that we are an island nation surrounded by the sea; that over 90% of our bulk commodities pass on the sea; that we are dependent on the sea for our economic survival in peace and our actual survival in war.

We neglect the sea at our peril. As early as 210 BC Themistocles wrote 'who controls the sea controls all'; the continuing relevance of this is clear to all thinking people, not least the potential enemy. And so to the Royal Navy and how it goes about its business, in conjunction with the other two Services and our NATO allies to keep the peace by deterring war.

I hope you will enjoy reading this book and will experience a rightful feeling of personal pride when you do so. It is written for you and tells you about your people; your ships, aircraft and submarines; your security – *your Navy*.

Preface

On 25 June 1981 Her Majesty's Government announced, in its White Paper *The United Kingdom Defence Programme: The Way Forward*, considerable planned changes to the structure of the Royal Navy in the decade ahead. It has been possible to take account of these plans in the 'Future' sections of each chapter of this book, but I have left the remainder of the language largely untouched since it is, after all, a document of record: this is how the Navy is in late 1981.

Those alterations notwithstanding, I think it is worth discussing in this Preface what may be the implications of the changes outlined in the White Paper. I must limit myself here, for I doubt if I am qualified – or allowed, come to that – to comment on the possible political effects. There will be such effects both internal and external, particularly in NATO, but I shall leave that to the press and the analysts. The implications that belong to this book are of two kinds: operational and organisational.

Operationally, we have to consider the effect of a reduction over the decade of nearly 20% in the destroyers and frigates ready for NATO tasks; this figure will be worse if many of the ships are in the Stand-by Squadron. In addition, there may be fewer decks for heavy anti-submarine helicopters available at sea. On the other hand, numbers of Fleet submarines will build up as previously planned, and long-range maritime patrol aircraft will be improved (again, as previously planned) and their numbers slightly increased.

These changes will have the effect of moving the focus of anti-submarine operations forward, away from any likely reinforcement route and towards the 'choke point' of the Greenland-Iceland-UK gap. They will mean that an opposing submarine which penetrates into the Eastern Atlantic has less stiff resistance in and around the reinforcement route than previous plans would have given it. On the other hand, its chances of penetration may be slightly less.

The question here is whether – discounting for a moment the capabilities of other navies which may be co-operating – British maritime forces of the shape now projected are properly balanced as between distant support and barrier operations, and operations around the reinforcement shipping that needs protection. It is worth reiterating that the Royal Navy is already more heavily balanced towards submarines than any other in the Western world; the next decade, on present plans, will shift that balance a great deal further.

Furthermore, air defence against a predominantly missile-armed enemy will inevitably be thinner than previous plans allowed, though there may be more chance of attrition by shorebased aircraft which are being slightly augmented. And finally, the moral support which surface craft give to unarmed merchantmen is not of negligible account.

Operationally, then, there is a judgment to be made as to whether the new plans cater sufficiently for that defence-in-depth which has been a hallmark of effective shipping protection in the past. I hope some of the facts and reasoning in later parts of this book will help readers to form such a judgment. To a degree, after nearly 40 years with great technical change and no major maritime war, we are all amateurs now, however hard and long some of us have studied these matters.

The organisational problem is that of running a Navy with a much higher proportion of its people embarked in ships. This is absolutely necessary to keep up force levels on the money we have been allotted. It means that much more training must go on at sea, when previously officers and men were brought to a high level of efficiency by shore training before joining a ship. It means less time for ships in dockyard hands, with greater theoretical chances of defects and fewer chances of the operational enhancement that fitting new designs or types of equipment can bring; though there should be some improvement in ship availability. It means increased need for careful management to avoid excessive hardships of family separation and turbulence. These may all seem to be minor administrative problems, but they are not. If stability and a reasonable run of planning can be assured, good management will probably cope with them, and a lean sharp Fleet will result. But if they are overlaid by short-term changes, particularly those that are imposed by budgetary considerations, they may be very damaging.

But provided that goes even reasonably well, by the end of the decade the United Kingdom will still have the third most powerful Navy in the world. One can say that with confidence, particularly, because simple arithmetic shows not far short of 20 nuclear-powered Fleet submarines in service by the end of 1991. No navy other than those of the USA and USSR will have more than a very few; and as this book shows, such vessels are the most potent maritime war-fighting units now available. Nor will the Royal Navy's surface Fleet or shipborne air power be less than substantial: sufficient, certainly, for the peacetime and low-intensity operations which – under the deterrent umbrella – naval forces actually *do*. Finally, the Royal Navy still has responsibility for the strategic nuclear deterrent, which occupies a very important place in current defence policy.

So there is a Tomorrow. It has more shreds and patches than some of us, including myself, would want, and it poses a considerable challenge to our management. But the job is vastly worthwhile, a core task of British defence, and the Royal Navy will cheerfully do the best it can with what it's got, while continuing to put its case for necessary improvements. May you live in interesting times, runs the ancient Chinese curse; looking back at our history, I doubt if we have ever lived in anything else. That tenacity which has been a hallmark of the Navy for so long is needed as much as ever, and will be forthcoming, as ever. There is a Tomorrow, all right.

Introduction

There is no better way of learning about one's own Service than writing a book about it. In my research I have been helped by very many busy people who have given me time, information and advice. My thanks are due to them all, and I should particularly name (in the order of the Chapters with which they helped) Professor Bryan Ranft; Vice-Admiral Sir William Staveley; Captain Frank Grenier; Commanders Mike Gretton and Jeremy Blackham; Rear-Admiral Edward Anson and his staff; Colonel Martin Garrod, Miss Bridget Spiers, Major Alastair Donald, Captains Derek Oakley and David Tong, and Sergeant Jones; Commander Bobby Pinson; Captains William Gueterbock and Toby Frere; Commandant Elizabeth Craig McFeeley, Superintendent Patricia Swallow and Second Officer Evelyn Strouts; Admiral Sir Desmond Cassidi, Rear-Admirals William Waddell and David Eckersley-Maslin, Captains Julian Oswald, Michael Vallis and Peter Wright; Rear-Admiral Peter Herbert and Captain David Morse; Commander Bob Davis and Mrs Pat Brown; Captain John Webster.

Photographs and illustrations are an integral part of the book and here too I have been lucky. Mr Stuart Reed and after him Mr John Margetts, and their staff, in the Ministry of Defence were immensely helpful and provided a large proportion of the photographs; others who gave a great deal of time and trouble were Lieutenant-Commander Coombes and Leading Wren Dee Walker at HMS *Excellent*; Lieutenant Ward and LWEM Carr of the RN Presentation Team; Captain Michael Livesay, Lieutenant-Commander Park and CPO Chant of HMS *Invincible*; Mr Charles Risk of BRNC Dartmouth; FCPO Troth and the photographic staff of the Directorate of Public Relations (Navy); Petty Officer Tierney of 800 Squadron; Mr Laurence Phillips and CPO Smart of the Commander-in-Chief, Fleet's staff. The National Maritime Museum, Imperial War Museum and many firms, all I hope acknowledged in the captions, very kindly made pictures available for reproduction.

Finally, there were some people who helped throughout the production of the book and need special acknowledgement: Captain Tony Collins, Commander Rex Phillips and Mr Joe Dodman of the Directorate of Public Relations (Navy); the staff of the Ministry of Defence Library; and Group Captain Alan Hollingsworth and all those concerned at Ian Allan.

Much of the merit in the book belongs to all these people; the mistakes are mine.

1

Some History

Time future is, as naval planners continually discover, contained in time past. At any given moment a navy is an inheritance not only of hardware and men but of history, traditions, methods and concepts; it is also an amalgam of plans and projects for time to come; it requires, in the nature of things, continuity between these. Thus, although this book is about the Royal Navy today and tomorrow, some historical introduction is necessary.

An island state looks at the sea in several ways. It is a sort of extended frontier across which invasion has to come if it comes at all. It is a hinterland that can provide economic wealth. And it is a means of access – until the appearance of air travel, the only physical access – to trade, wealth, power and influence in the places beyond it.

Britain has looked at the sea in all these ways, often simultaneously. Between the first and twelfth centuries the invasion aspect was certainly uppermost. Colonising Romans, marauding Danes and Norsemen, and invading Saxons and Normans demonstrated that an island without means of resistance in its sea approaches is little less vulnerable than a state with land frontiers. When, rarely, a unifying king could be found in England who also appreciated the importance of strength at sea, then some check to assault from seaward was possible. Because Alfred the Great was such a king he is sometimes regarded as having founded the Royal Navy. But his lessons were forgotten, to the extent that 200 years later the lack of permanent English naval forces was an important factor in William the Conqueror's success. Shortly before William's invasion, Harold Godwinson's temporarily gathered fleet dispersed because there was no food or pay for the men.

In the Middle Ages a new pattern emerged of a nucleus of a few King's Ships which were joined in time of need by a sort of maritime *levée en masse*. This was made easier by the fact that merchant and war vessels were not sharply differentiated, their main function in war being to carry soldiers and their main fighting method being boarding. Such fleets defeated French invasion attempts at the battles of South Foreland in 1217 and Sluys in 1340. In the first of these the French fleet was under way; in the second it was at anchor. In both cases, the English forces used their mobility to concentrate and press home the attack.

From about 1500 onwards the ad hoc nature of the Medieval fleet began gradually to give place to the more formalised structure of a national maritime force. There were two main reasons for this. First, technology – particularly the mounting of large cannon in the broadsides of increasingly large ships – was changing the nature of sea-fighting, making it more specialised and professional, and differentiating somewhat more sharply between merchant and war vessels. Secondly, there was a stronger grasp of the advantages to an island nation of maximum use of the sea and, conversely, of the dangers of neglecting sea defences. The famous 'Libel of English Policy', a verse treatise of about 1436, said

> Keep then the sea that is the wall of England
> And then is England kept by Goddes hand.

But the work contains more than that succinct summary. Its analysis is both strategic and economic. It was probably the first

Above: In medieval sea-fighting ships were used as infantry carriers. In this battle (La Rochelle, 1372) the English were defeated.
National Maritime Museum

'Role-of-the-Navy' paper, but it was also a polemic for maritime power in general.

So, up to the end of the 16th century, sponsored by far-sighted rulers of whom Henry VII and Henry VIII were the most prominent, England's sea interests and power expanded vastly. Voyages of exploration and trade by merchant adventurers, increases in the size and number of royal ships, and rapid advances in the techniques of navigation and sea-fighting were characteristics of the period. There was still, of course, great flexibility in organisation and structure. Merchant ships commonly had to fight their way into trading patterns against Spanish or Portuguese claims to monopoly, officers fulfilling royal commissions for a single voyage would revert to a private role in their next, and in the defeat of the Spanish Armada the

Left: A ship of the Armada period: guns were now mounted in the broadside and battering power became an important component of sea-fighting. *National Maritime Museum*

Below: A contemporary plan of the later stages of the Armada action, 1588. Fighting was now effective in the open sea as well as in coastal waters. *National Maritime Museum*

Right: Sir Francis Drake. *National Maritime Museum*

Below right: A contemporary model of the Commonwealth ship *Naseby*, 1655. Battleship design altered only in detail for the next 200 years. *National Maritime Museum*

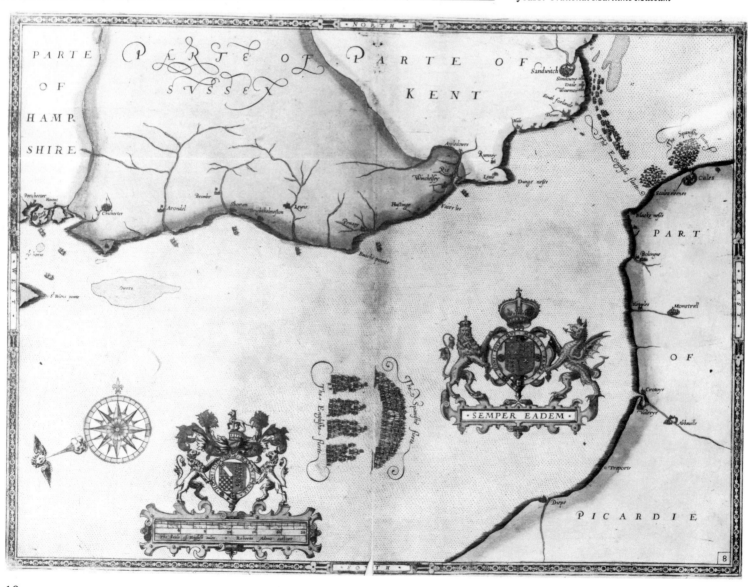

maritime *levée en masse* was again employed, 34 royal ships being joined by over 100 from the merchant fleet. The Armada campaign was, for the English, a triumph of ad hoc organisation, command and control, and tactical ingenuity combined with prudence: careful harrying and pursuit up the Channel, the assault of the fireships at Calais, the shattering fight off Gravelines all substantiate this claim. God, it is true, then 'blew with his winds and they were scattered'; He but finished the 'great matter' that Howard and Drake had endeavoured.

Under the Stuarts, from 1603 to 1640, maritime trade continued to expand, with increasing competition from the Dutch. The Royal Navy declined under James I, and Charles I's expensive attempts to revive it constituted one factor in the political, economic, social and religious pressures that led to the Civil War. But there is some doubt about what Charles I was trying to do with sea power. He certainly had very strong ideas about maritime sovereignty; he laid claim to extensive areas in the Channel and round the coast, he sponsored Selden's book '*Mare Clausum*' as a reply to the Dutchman Grotius's claim to freedom of the seas in '*Mare Liberum*', and he instituted fishery protection patrols with his Ship-money fleet. It appears (Charles's language was notoriously opaque) that he viewed the Royal Navy as primarily a protection force for what we would nowadays call an 'Exclusive Economic Zone'.

Cromwell and the later Stuarts had less theoretical ideas. The Dutch challenge remained. Cromwell's 'Western Design', which turned British policy towards gaining 'an interest in that part of the West Indies in the possession of the Spaniards', was also an instrument for containing Dutch trade expansion and taking from them the leadership of the Protestant interest. His strategy was bound to lead to war with the Dutch sooner or later; paradoxically, when it came the *casus belli* was precisely a Dutch

abrogation of the closed-sea doctrine that Cromwell had already tacitly relinquished. In 1652 Tromp the elder failed to salute the flag of Dover Castle and later that of Admiral Blake, and a battle ensued which, like so many in the Dutch wars, ended with no decisive advantage to either side.

Nevertheless – and in spite of the excellent seamanship and fighting qualities of the Dutch, particularly their outstanding Admiral de Ruyter – these wars ended with what must be acknowledged the defeat of the Dutch in 1674, a year still called in that country the *rampjaar* or year of disaster. It was a case of a small power, composed in any case of city-states, being ground down by a combination of enemies each of whom had a more centralised direction and broader economic base.

The Dutch wars brought on, as wars tend to do, advances in technology, tactics and organisation in the Royal Navy. It was now recognisably a permanent national force. Actions were fought by specialised fighting ships; merchant ships fought only in self-defence, and in dangerous waters expected to be convoyed. Ship design, in the hands of Phineas and Peter Pett, a most effective father-and-son team, made great advances, to the extent that the fighting and handling qualities of a battleship scarcely altered for the next two centuries. With this standardisation of design came a formalisation of tactics. Now that the great gun, with its battering power, was the primary weapon at sea, it had to be used to the maximum advantage; and, since it was mounted in the broadside, this led clearly to the institution of the line-ahead, or line of battle, as the primary fighting formation. The best thing an individual ship could do in battle was to cross her opponent's bow or stern and 'rake' her with a full broadside; the worst thing she could do was allow herself to be raked; thus, in fleet actions, allowing the enemy to break the line was a cardinal sin. The British learnt this early, incorporated it in the Fighting Instructions of 1653, and used it particularly effectively in the Four Days' Battle of 1666 during the Second Dutch War. Finally, in this era of ordering and formalisation (it was, after all, the century of Descartes and Newton) the Royal Navy found its organiser in Samuel Pepys. This great Secretary to the Admiralty reformed the procurement, provisioning, pay, officer structure and secretarial practices of the Navy. By the time he left office in 1689, it was a well-ordered and professional force and its administration rested on a sound basis.

The foundations were now laid for the classical course of British policy: ensuring that no continental power dominated Europe, and concurrently expanding overseas trade and possessions. Inevitably this led to conflict with France, and from 1690 to 1815 France was a consistent opponent in a series of wars in which the other protagonists changed sides frequently.

They did not start too auspiciously for Britain or for the Royal Navy. But a considerable French success off Beachy Head in 1690 was not followed up; while a partial British victory in 1692 off Barfleur was capped by the destruction of much of Tourville's exhausted and outnumbered fleet at anchor round La Hougue. This series of battles helps to indicate the pattern of the 18th century conflict at sea. For much of the period the British were matched in nearly every quality: discipline, professionalism, ship technology, courage; but they always excelled in one: tenacity. When that tenacity could be harnessed by tactical commanders with offensive flair, such as Rooke, Hawke and pre-eminently Nelson, it proved decisive. When lesser mortals disposed of it, it just meant not losing; holding what had been gained; protecting the trade which invariably continued throughout these wars; and constricting the trade of opponents as well as the movements of their fleets.

Thus, throughout the Wars of the Spanish Succession (1702-1713) and the Austrian Succession (1739-1748), the Seven Years'

Below: The Battle of La Hougue, 1692: Rooke's boats going in to attack the exhausted French Fleet. *National Maritime Museum*

Right: The Battle of Quiberon Bay, 1759. Paton, the artist, shows the moment when the French ship *Thesée* (left centre), her gunports open, foundered in the force 9 gale. *National Maritime Museum*

Below right: 'The Liberty of the Subject': Gillray's acid comment on the pressgang as a method of recruitment. *National Maritime Museum*

13

War (1756-1763) and – less successfully because there was no distraction on the Continent for European enemies – the War of American Independence (1775-1783), the sea power of Britain was an essential element of policy for the defence of British territory, the preservation of the balance of power in Europe, and the protection and expansion of British interests overseas. British naval power and the economic strength of the country were mutually reinforcing and seen to be so; therefore, though the Navy was often allowed to decline, it was never totally neglected. The policy reached its culmination in the Napoleonic Wars (1793-1815) which left British power, and particularly naval power, unchallenged for nearly a century thereafter.

It was not achieved without cost. Life in the Royal Navy was in many aspects harsh and dangerous. The officers, certainly, had reasonable if cramped conditions, just adequate pay when afloat, and the prospect of putting together considerable fortunes from prize money if they were lucky. The ratings, more than half of them conscripted by the rough and ready mechanism of the press-gang, lived by their guns in extremely crowded and unhygienic conditions, feeding when at sea on salt beef and biscuit and precious little else except rum. Discipline was rigorous, and punishments by modern standards brutal; flogging was commonplace. Disease was a more common killer than battle; ships at sea for long periods were particularly subject to scurvy, which for example killed 1300 of Anson's 1500 men during his circumnavigation of 1740-1744.

How on earth was so barbarously managed a Service able to achieve such success? There seem to be two sides to the answer. First, no one should be deceived by the prettiness of 18th century art into thinking it was a pretty age, ashore or afloat. Gillray is probably truer to life than Sayer. But secondly, there is much evidence of real humanity and care, and true leadership, in the great bulk of ships of the Fleet. Captains were constantly on the look out for opportunities to get fresh provisions; the long days and weeks at sea, even on blockade duty, were occupied in drills to improve fighting and sailing efficiency, signalling and manoeuvring; professional education was not neglected; hygiene

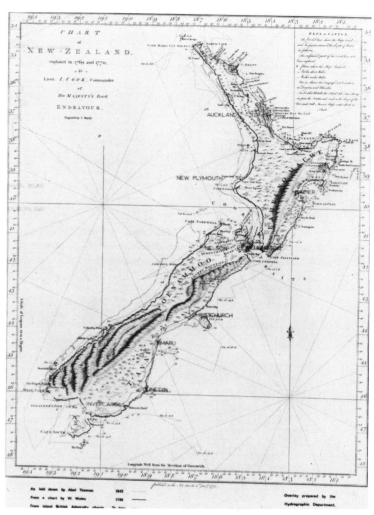

Above: Enduring standards of accuracy: Cook's chart of New Zealand, 1770. *National Maritime Museum*

Left: A prettier view of the eighteenth-century sailor's life: 'Jack Oakham throws out a signal for an engagement' by Sayer. *National Maritime Museum*

Right: Captain James Cook, by Nathaniel Dance. *National Maritime Museum*

was as good as could be managed. In most ships the chain of command, from the captain through the officers to the petty officers and seamen, was firm and unbroken, with the physical proximity of all to each other, and shared danger, acting as powerful bonds. Of course there were desertions, and disciplinary problems, of which the mutinies of 1797 were the most serious: but the underlying spirit of the eighteenth-century Navy was one of confidence, patriotism and mutual trust.

Certainly there were some checks and reverses: in sea-fighting, they were caused generally by too slavish a following of the line-of-battle doctrine in the Fighting Instructions; in amphibious operations, by inadequate preparation and misunderstanding between sailors and soldiers. But the successes were many; in 1759, 'the wonderful year', so many indeed that the victory of Hawke at Quiberon Bay (in a force nine gale!) has tended to eclipse the scarcely less notable exploits of Boscawen at Lagos and Saunders at Quebec. But of all the successful men of the 18th-century Navy two names particularly stand out: James Cook and Horatio Nelson.

Cook came to the Navy as a lower-deck volunteer after serving in North Sea colliers. By sheer ability he rose through the rank of master (or navigator) to commander to captain; and in the course of this he carried out his three great voyages of discovery to the Pacific. He set standards in the accuracy of hydrographic surveying that have endured to the present day. His enterprise

and spirit of scientific enquiry were matched by consistency of purpose. His care for his ship's companies' conditions and hygiene was so good that in his first voyage not a man died from scurvy. (Ironically, this set back the discovery of citrus fruits or other vitamin C-rich food as the remedy for the disease, since Cook had been charged with investigating as a specific the use of wort of malt and sauerkraut, neither of which contain any vitamin C to speak of.) The man, and his work, were universally admired and respected; the French Navy was instructed not to molest him.

Nelson's career is too well known to be detailed here. His parsonage upbringing was, to be sure, a trifle misleading; the influence of well-to-do naval relations had something to do with his early advancement. But his ability, his swift appreciation of problems, and more than anything his ardour for battle and glory, were more powerful motors. As commodore and admiral, his success in battle was unparalleled and protean: his brilliant and brave manoeuvre at St Vincent, his cool seizure of an opportunity for annihilation (a favourite word of his) at the Nile, his gutsy slogging-match at Copenhagen not to mention his diplomacy after it, his vigil on the prolonged and wearing blockade of Toulon, and the culmination of it all at Trafalgar, showed him as a master of all the tactical maritime arts. He was vain, ebullient, full of human foibles and frailties: the Fleet loved him for them almost as much as for his courage and skill.

These two men, Cook and Nelson, were about as different in character as it is possible to conceive. Yet the Royal Navy accommodated them both, even though neither was in its classic mould. And they shared qualities which, as intelligent men, they had learnt from naval service: a vast and comprehensive professionalism; immense attention to detail; and constant care for the men under their command. Those lessons are re-learnt by every generation of naval officers, then, today, and tomorrow.

In the 19th century the Royal Navy faced an enormous variety of problems. It was, of course, pre-eminent, the instrument of Pax Britannica, and one of the chief motors of Empire. Its problems were far more those of new technological, administrative and social practices than of fighting mortal

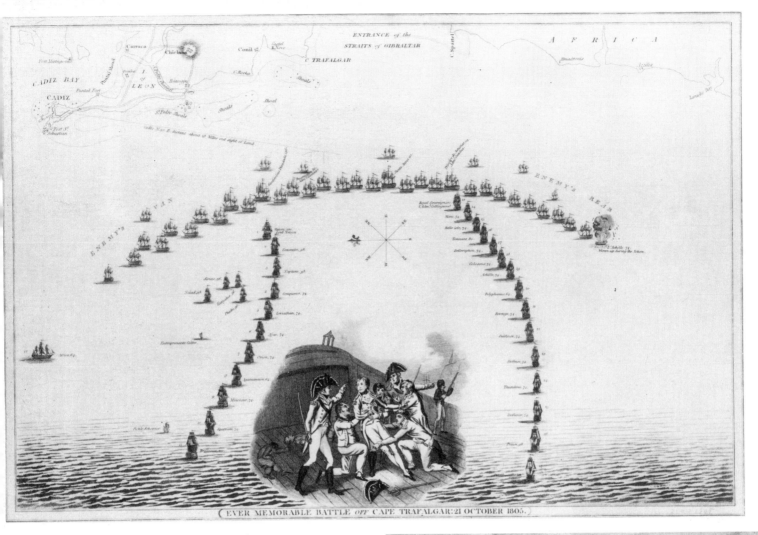

(EVER MEMORABLE BATTLE off CAPE TRAFALGAR: 21 OCTOBER 1805.)

Above left: Viscount Nelson, by Abbott. *National Maritime Museum*

Left: The Battle of the Nile: the French flagship, *L'Orient*, blowing up. *National Maritime Museum*

Above: The Battle of Trafalgar: a contemporary print showing Nelson's plan. *National Maritime Museum*

Right: HMS *Captain*: a tragically unsuccessful design of the 1860s. Note the turret guns, full sailing rig and low freeboard. *National Maritime Museum*

Below right: HMS *Devastation*: only three years later than the *Captain*, the archetypal armoured battleship. *National Maritime Museum*

enemies – though examples of small-scale actions, often involving outstanding coolness and courage against great odds, are numerous.

Technically, the Navy had to move from wood and sail and cannonballs to steel and steam and shells. Each of these was a revolution, and for the largest navy in the world – and therefore the one with the greatest vested interest in the *status quo* – to manage all three in well under a century was in fact good going. Naturally there were many false starts and wrong turnings, and some unjustified hankering after old ways: an attempt to incorporate a full sailing rig in a ship mounting heavy gun-turrets (HMS *Captain*, 1870) is perhaps the maddest example, and tragic too, for she capsized with her designer and most of her crew. In the same year was laid down a much more soundly-conceived vessel, HMS *Devastation*. With turret guns and steam power only, she was in effect the prototype battleship. With improvements in armour, propulsion and armament, the development of battleships runs clear from this vessel to the last of the breed.

Smaller types of ship gave more scope for both innovation and nostalgic retention of old techniques. The latter, to be sure, were

Right: The old order and the new: submarines passing **HMS** *Dreadnought*, 1906.
National Maritime Museum

Below: The development of naval aviation was the chief innovation in the Fleet between the wars. **Fairy IIIFs** over HMS *Courageous* in the Mediterranean. *Imperial War Museum*

Bottom right: Maintenance of standards ensured a highly-tuned Service on entry into World War II. Mediterranean Fleet destroyers and submarines in the mid-1930s. *Imperial War Museum*

often needed because in the corners of the world where these ships operated, no coal or technical support was to be had. Nevertheless, by the turn of the century the Fleet was a hotchpotch of diverse classes of ship, with no clear concept of operations and much dead wood. And a challenge was fast emerging from Germany – hungry for Empire, untrammelled by tradition or possessions, technically advanced. The Royal Navy, prestigious, well-disciplined and – after a series of much-needed reforms from the 1860s onwards – well-officered and manned, needed a strong man to point the way.

It found one in Admiral 'Jacky' Fisher, a character several times larger than life. His reforms and rationalisations between 1900 and 1910 shook down the Navy into a balanced, very powerful battle fleet with the bulk of other naval forces structured to serve that fleet's purposes. Conceptually, it owed a good deal to the American Admiral Mahan's theories of sea power, particularly on the pre-eminence of fleet action. Technically, it owed much to the all-big-gun theories of such innovators as Cuniberti. But its organisation and structure were Fisher's own, and its mission clear: to counter the German High Seas Fleet and defeat it if it ventured to break out. The defects were of Fisher's making too: over-centralisation of command and control, unwillingness of subordinates to exercise tactical initiative, and a certain tendency – brought on by Fisher's idiosyncratic way of conducting business as well as by his famous controversy with Lord Charles Beresford – to cliquiness and intrigue.

In World War I, the Fleet's only action at Jutland, where with a preponderance of 37 capital ships to 27 the British could only drive the Germans back to their base with little loss, demonstrated these defects as well as some material shortcomings in the British battlecruisers (three were lost) and armour-piercing shell. Admiral Sir John Jellicoe, the Commander-in-Chief, has been criticised for his cautious handling of the Grand Fleet. But he was, after all, 'the only man who could have lost the War in an afternoon'; no one had ever fought an action of this scale, with such ships or equipment, before; the effects of a melee, particularly in poor visibility or at night, were unpredictable. As it was, British casualties were greater than at Trafalgar; but the German High Seas Fleet did not seek battle again.

But the guns at Jutland, newly in action though they were, sounded the finale of the great battles between lines of ships. They were already giving place to two new elements of maritime warfare: the submarine and the aircraft.

Some elements in Germany, seeing her as likely to remain the weaker naval power, had always been drawn towards attacking Allied commerce – the classical *guerre de course*. The implementation of this policy by unrestricted submarine warfare ran the risk of direct confrontation with the USA, which was still neutral at the time, because it infringed the USA's cherished claim to freedom of the seas. It was, therefore, embarked on only reluctantly; but after several reversals of policy, the Germans conducted unrestricted U-boat warfare without a break from early 1917 to the end of the war. It posed a very severe threat to Britain, and the institution of mercantile convoy from mid-1917 came only just in time. Both submarine and anti-submarine methods were still fairly crude, with much use of surface gunfire – partly, in the case of the submarines, to conserve torpedoes – and the concentration of merchant ships with some sort of escort was enough to defeat the submarines even though underwater detection scarcely existed.

As for aircraft, their maritime roles in World War I involved a good deal of scouting and reconnaissance, with limited offensive operations mounted from shore particularly in overseas theatres. Their time was to come.

Indeed, the development of maritime forces between 1918 and 1939 concerned mainly the use of aircraft, particularly carrier-based aircraft (Britain had conducted the first deck-landing in 1917, but generally lagged behind the USA in aircraft-carrier techniques), and countering submarines. The development of underwater detection and attack methods, particularly from destroyer-sized ships, gave the Navy a good deal of confidence in the anti-submarine field on entering World War II.

So, of course, did the fact that financial stringency, very severe in the 1920s and early 1930s, had been relaxed and much new construction was under way; and so did the excellent leadership and management which Admiral of the Fleet Lord Chatfield had given in the late 1930s. He may have paid too much attention to battleship construction, but his retrieval of control of the Fleet Air Arm, which had been lost on the formation of the Royal Air Force in 1919, was a necessary first step in the further development of the air side of the Service and he could hardly have moved more rapidly in that area.

The Royal Navy in World War II was, therefore, very much an all-arms maritime force and it is notable how few campaigns, or even single actions, were waged by forces of one kind alone. The attack on the Italian Fleet at Taranto, to be sure, may stand as a monument to carrier-based air forces; and the destruction of the *Scharnhorst* off North Cape, in the long Boxing Day night of 1943, to surface forces alone. But by and large, the aircraft was a necessary component of all maritime operations, whether in the anti-submarine battles of the Atlantic and Arctic convoys, the anti-surface ship engagements of the *Bismarck* and Cape Matapan, the fighting through to Malta of convoys against air opposition, the numerous large-scale amphibious operations that were a characteristic of the war, and the British Pacific Fleet's participation in the final US operations against Japan. The integration of submarines into operations was a good deal less close, but they played a prominent part particularly in the Mediterranean campaign, and the threat of their presence in all theatres affected the plans and operations of both sides.

There was one further new element in the all-arms Navy. As Sir Henry Tizard once pointed out, major changes in sea warfare since 1900 were wrought not only by the aircraft and the submarine, but by the electron. The introduction before the war of Asdic (later called sonar) for detecting submerged submarines provided a reliable basis for anti-submarine operations particularly round convoys; the invention and rapid development of radar for detecting and tracking both surface and aircraft targets meant that by 1942 many problems of long-distance above-water warfare, in all weathers, could be solved, and that the surface of the sea could be denied to submarines when any radars whether sea- or air-borne were about. Radio communications, used but rudimentary in World War I, were vastly expanded; so of course were the attendant risks of detection and location by interception and direction-finding equipment, and compromise of plans by the deciphering of messages. In all these applications of electronic technology the Royal Navy was in the first rank of competence, able to exploit any mistakes and shortcomings of an opponent.

The Royal Navy, then, ended World War II as a very successful service. It had fought and won one vital battle, in the Atlantic, and any number of vastly important ones. It had proved itself capable of nearly tenfold expansion (its wartime strength was 863,500) and very difficult feats of organisation in the naval control of shipping and mounting of amphibious operations. It had remained in the forefront of technology. Most of all, it had proved over and over again its courage and tenacity.

It now had to move into a rapidly changing, difficult and still dangerous world. With resources that were in any case limited and diminished with the relative worsening of the country's economy, with shrinking imperial commitments and expanding alliance concerns, and above all with the realities of the atomic age and the existence of superpowers: with all these, it had to come to terms. How it has done so, in terms both of its role and the instruments it uses to fulfil that role, is the theme of the rest of this book.

Below: A convoy in the Atlantic during World War II. The Battle of the Atlantic was the Royal Navy's most crucial of the war, and most of the ingredients of victory are represented in this picture: surface escorts, aircraft both land and sea based, and not least the staunch and courageous Merchant Marine. *Imperial War Museum*

The Task

In common with the whole of British strategy, the task of the Royal Navy has undergone much reappraisal in the past decade or two. While no single, authoritative, up-to-date description of the task exists, it is possible to derive from Defence White Papers and the statements of senior officers a reasonable summary of it. The terms in which it is expressed are, however, the author's own.

First, it is plain that the task of the Royal Navy must be compatible with the strategy of the United Kingdom as a whole. This, as the steady refinement of language during successive Defence White Papers of the 1970s suggests, is now relatively settled. The United Kingdom has chosen to safeguard its vital interests – territorial integrity, political independence and economic viability – against external military threat, by membership of the North Atlantic Treaty Organisation; and its contribution to the forces of NATO is the major determinant of its defence planning.

But under that very broad rubric the special characteristics of a contributing power, and particularly of a major medium-power contributor like the United Kingdom, will be important factors. One of the most salient characteristics of the UK is its dependence on the maritime aspects of its economy. Nearly 30% of the value of Britain's gross national product each year is represented by its seaborne trade; this figure is higher by a factor of three than that of any NATO partner except the Netherlands. Similarly, the UK-flag merchant fleet is, apart from that of Greece, the largest in NATO. Moreover, Britain's fuel sources, though closer to home than they were, are still sea-based.

All this adds up to a lot of economic stake at sea, and corresponding vulnerability if that stake is threatened. It would therefore be surprising if Britain's contribution to its alliance did not include a relatively high proportion of maritime forces. There are three other factors which reinforce this reasoning. First, the position of Great Britain at, so to speak, the sea-gate of Europe gives it a unique strategic place in any transatlantic defence structure. The key aspect of that structure is that the power of the United States should be brought to the aid of the continent of Europe in time of need; by convincing the Soviet Union that this can be done, the Alliance deters the main threat to it. It would be an odd world in which any but the Royal Navy played the major part in the approaches to that sea-gate. Second, Britain has chosen to continue its deployment of an independent strategic nuclear deterrent, as a contribution to the strategic forces of the Alliance, but with the particular quality that attaches to a second centre of nuclear decision-making operationally quite independent of the USA. This deterrent is deployed at sea. Finally, the UK has outside the NATO area – which extends in the Atlantic only as far as the Tropic of Cancer – politico-military interests of various kinds. Some are, to put it bluntly, the residue of Empire, like Belize and Hong Kong; others are Commonwealth bonds of unwritten association, as with Australia and Kenya; yet others are mutually beneficial relationships like that with Oman. The last two sorts, particularly, are of benefit to the West as well as to Britain alone, and all can be fostered by the backing and occasional appearance of British maritime power.

In common with its NATO partners, the UK is bound to see the principal threat at present as coming from the Soviet Union. The Soviet Navy and Naval Air Force have developed into a formidable fighting instrument, with emphasis on submarines, long-range tactical strike aircraft, and heavily-armed surface units. All arms make use of tactical missiles, mainly for anti-ship purposes and with ranges up to some hundreds of miles. All the evidence suggests that while 20 and even 10 years ago the Soviet objective was to deny the use of the sea to the West, now they also consider the possibility of using the sea to project power, and not only strategic deterrent power, far beyond their borders.

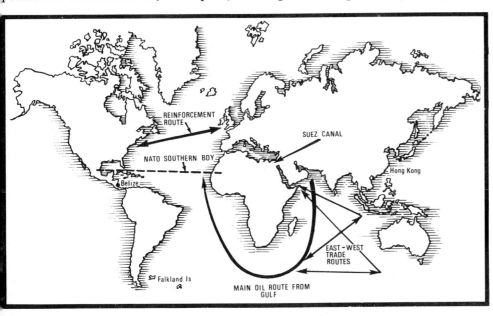

Left: The NATO sea area, and Western maritime interests outside it. Some British post-imperial commitments are also indicated.

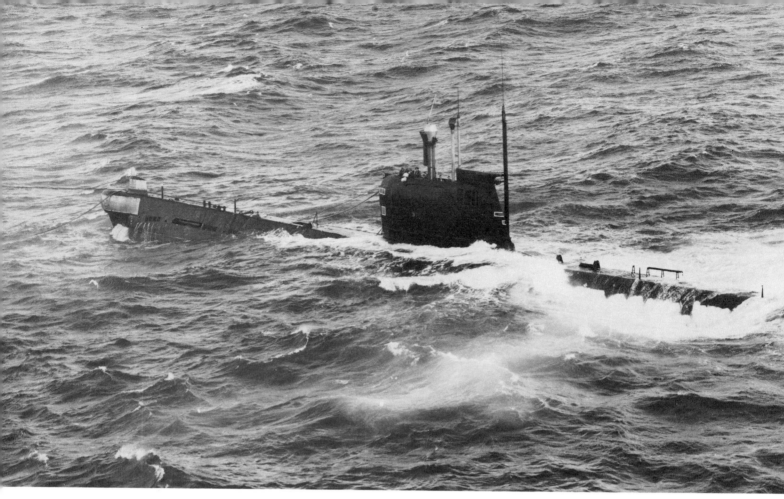

There are of course other threats, much smaller in scale but perhaps, in the nature of the modern world where superpower weighs heavily but moves cautiously, more likely to be used. Typically these come from nations equipped with Soviet-built vessels and weaponry including tactical missiles: forces of relatively short reach and mainly suitable for sea-denial operations against forces of their own weight or against merchant shipping. In such conditions they are capable of many levels of force, from harassment through gunfire to missile and torpedo attack. In the numerous events of the last decade where such forces have been used – the Indo-Pakistan War of 1971, the Yom Kippur War of 1973, the Iraq-Iran war of 1980 are but three – there has not been great physical damage to Western shipping; but this may be at least as much due to the deterrent effect of Western naval forces as to the restraint of participants.

For, of course, deterrence is not confined to strategic rivalry between the superpowers. It operates at all levels of potential conflict and in all environments. It operates sometimes by the presence of a single national unit, appropriately backed; sometimes by a whole complex structure of alliances and forces that will confront an opponent with a thicket of unpleasant possibilities that he cannot brush aside. It must, indeed, as NATO doctrine states, be a system of flexible response (and maritime forces, given their mobility and command of varying levels of firepower, are peculiarly flexible instruments). But it will always have one objective: to persuade a potential opponent that a military course of action will be unprofitable for him.

It would be nice, of course, if international affairs could be so regulated that all this machinery was unnecessary. Some commentators have seen the Law of the Sea conference as an opportunity to establish such an international regime at sea, perhaps even confining maritime forces to 'economic zones' off the coasts of their own countries. But, desirable though a Law of the Sea Convention is, it is quite unlikely to eliminate either legal disputes at sea or the perceptions of the larger states that the sea is a necessary environment for projecting power. Moreover, international regulation presupposes international policing, and there is no sign of such a development. So national forces, moving in relative freedom, will remain arbiters at sea for the foreseeable future.

Left: A Soviet *Foxtrot*-Class submarine, one of over 200 conventionally-powered Soviet boats, in the Mediterranean. The photograph was taken by a Sea King helicopter of 826 Squadron; the downwash of the helicopter's rotor can be seen in the foreground of the picture.
Crown Copyright

Below left: A Soviet *Charlie*-Class submarine. These are nuclear-propelled submarines capable of firing anti-ship guided missiles from ranges out to 25 miles or so. The hydrodynamically efficient 'pear-drop' hull form can be clearly seen.
Crown Copyright

Right: A *Krivak*-Class Soviet destroyer, with missile armament forward and guns aft, refuelling in the English Channel. Photograph by a Sea King helicopter of 820 Squadron. *Crown Copyright*

Below: A Soviet *Delta*-Class Ballistic Missile submarine. The range of the *Delta's* missiles enables it to threaten the USA from patrol stations in the Barents Sea.
Crown Copyright

Bottom: The Soviet amphibious ship *Ivan Rogov*, the first such Soviet ship to incorporate a docking well. She is of fully oceanic range and can operate helicopters, and represents a major advance in Soviet ability to project power ashore.
Crown Copyright

That, then, is the setting in which the Royal Navy must accomplish its task: as a major maritime contributor to a NATO alliance which is increasingly concerned about what goes on outside its area but is still predominantly occupied with the Soviet threat to Europe; viewing the Soviet Navy and naval air force as the governing threats when considering its force structure; mantaining the breadth and flexibility to exert a deterrent influence in a great variety of situations.

We can now look more closely at some of those situations to see how they may affect the make-up of the Royal Navy: always remembering that certain aspects of the maritime task fall to the Royal Air Force, and that both duplication and gaps in capability must be avoided. It is convenient to group situations under various levels of conflict: as will be apparent, conflict does not always involve shooting.

Normal Conditions

By definition, in normal conditions (which could also be called 'Peaceful Co-existence', but in the competitive interpretation used by the Soviet Union rather than any less robust definition current in the West) the situation is stable in the sense that tensions are well compensated, change is managed by negotiation, and vital interests are not being eroded or attacked. The corollary, in our power-directed world, is that deterrence is operating satisfactorily.

For the Royal Navy, this means several things. First and foremost, it is necessary to maintain the strategic nuclear deterrent on constant patrol, undetected in the ocean and thus capable with certainty of inflicting unacceptable damage on a nuclear aggressor. It has been explained in recent Government papers that such a 'bolt from the blue' aggression is a most unlikely contingency; but it is still worth guarding against it, and more importantly the blackmailing threat of it, by maintaining – as the UK has done since 1969 – a Polaris submarine constantly on patrol. That worst case being catered for, such a patrol can of course cope with any less time-urgent threats requiring strategic deterrence.

But for the rest of the Royal Navy there are many other tasks under normal conditions, and they still fall under the definition of deterrence. For in order to deter any shift from this desirable state of equilibrium, naval forces must be ready, and involved in the areas where it matters, and in sufficient numbers to check instabilities. They must also be capable – in case the calculations

Below: The Soviet aircraft carrier *Kiev*, with Hormone helicopters and Forger V/STOL aircraft on deck. Anti-submarine, anti-surface ship and anti-aircraft armament can be seen forward. The *Kiev* gives the Soviet Navy a focus, hitherto lacking, for comprehensive worldwide naval operations.
Crown Copyright

Left: A peacetime ship-visit: in September, 1980, three British warships paid the first Royal Naval visit to China for 30 years. Here the British Ambassador, Sir Percy Cradock, and Rear-Admiral D. C. Jenkin are welcomed by applauding Chinese ratings. *Crown Copyright*

Below: The United Kingdom's strategic nuclear deterrent is carried by four *Polaris* submarines, each of which has more firepower than all the bombs dropped by both sides in World War II. This photograph shows HMS *Revenge* at sea in the Clyde area. Once on patrol she is, of course, permanently submerged. *Crown Copyright*

Left: Offshore protection: naval divers embarked in a Gemini dinghy carry out an anti-sabotage check on a gas rig in the North Sea. *Crown Copyright*

Below: Offshore protection: HMS *Soberton* combines fishery protection and gas platform surveillance duties. *Crown Copyright*

Right: Surveillance: A Nimrod aircraft of the Royal Air Force keeps watch on a Soviet nuclear-powered guided missile submarine of the E-II class. RN/RAF co-operation in the maritime field is close and constantly exercised. *Crown Copyright*

Below right: Surveillance: a Soviet *Krivak*-Class destroyer from the flight deck of HMS *Norfolk*. *Crown Copyright*

are wrong – of reinforcement, so that any potential opponent can see no chance of an action on his part having any finality.

Naturally, visibility and mobility and a demonstrably high state of training are important characteristics of Naval forces doing this sort of low-level deterrent job, which is often summed up by the word 'presence'. Surface ships in particular provide such qualities; shipborne helicopters can greatly widen the area of influence of a single ship. But, of course, if a potential opponent knows that one of our submarines is about, that is also very helpful in deterrent terms. It should be emphasised that presence is usually a very discreet, peaceable occupation; and it includes winning friends – particularly by joint exercises, the relief of national disasters and goodwill visits – as well as influencing people. The velvet glove can be as thick as one pleases, and it is one of the pleasanter conventions of sea power that the mailed fist is seldom mentioned, much less exposed.

A particular form of presence, and one of a more overtly policing nature, is the patrol of offshore areas round the British Isles. This estate is immensely valuable both in living and non-living resources, and the maintenance of the United Kingdom's rights under international law in a zone of 200 miles and more offshore is a novel and growing task. Some specialised ships, such as diving craft and small submersibles, and some small patrol craft whose fighting qualities are minimal, are appropriate here.

Finally, there is a need to gather intelligence on, and conduct surveillance of, potential opponents. It requires a mixture of coarse and fine-grain systems that ideally include fixed installations, satellites, aircraft both shore and ship based, surface ships and submarines. The Royal Navy can provide some but not all of these, acting of course always within the limits of international law.

Low Intensity Operations

If deterrence breaks down, but not catastrophically, naval forces may move into low intensity operations. These never merit the title of war, are limited in aim, scope and area, and are generally governed by the international law of self-defence. This means that they will be conducted, so far as the Royal Navy is concerned, under carefully-drawn Rules of Engagement. They may, therefore, include sporadic shooting incidents but with limited weapon systems. The 1960s included numerous examples of the Royal Navy's involvement in such operations – of which the Beira Patrol, to stop oil illegally entering Rhodesia, was at the low end of the scale while the maritime element of the 'Confrontation' of Malaysia by Indonesia was at the high end. The 1970s gave us two 'Cod Wars' in a fishing dispute with Iceland, now happily concluded, an anti-gunrunning operation off Northern Ireland, and evacuation of civilians from Cyprus and Iran. In the early 1980s, the most significant such operation has been the surface patrol in the Gulf of Oman which has helped to stem any extension of the Iraq-Iran war to Western shipping.

It can be seen that such operations, as well as varying in scale and intensity, fall into two broad categories: sea use, which includes the protection of shipping against piracy or harassment, demonstrations of political resolve or legal right, the passage of military reinforcements, and the evacuation of civilians from dangerous areas; and sea denial, which includes counter-harassment and anti-gunrunning or anti-saboteur operations.

In all these circumstances there is a need for flexible and discriminating weapon systems that are capable of applying just enough force to achieve the aim. It is important to occupy a position in world public opinion squarely between the bully and the whipping-boy. For this task, surface ships are generally the best vehicles. Not only do they have the right range of weapons – some can even be fired to miss, and seen to be meant to miss – but they have more reliable communications and data acquisition systems than either submarines or fixed-wing aircraft. But this is not to say that the latter sorts of unit are of no value. Both are valuable cover against escalation; as examples, an opponent who knows that a British nuclear-powered submarine is about will think twice before using his surface forces to attack a British surface ship or group, and the presence of fixed-wing aircraft in

the area will have a similar effect as well as providing valuable surveillance potential. These more potent but less precisely discriminating units, then, are good sticks to shake; but the brunt of low-intensity operations will be borne by surface units, usually of medium size, and their embarked helicopters.

Operations at the Higher Level

Whether they evolve from low-intensity operations or are triggered directly by a major breakdown of deterrence, operations at the higher level can be defined as active hostilities involving on both sides fleet units and/or aircraft, with the use of major weapons. There may still be Rules of Engagement in an attempt to keep some limits on the conflict (there will certainly, for example, be absolute political control over the first use of tactical nuclear weapons) but these will be a good deal more relaxed than in low-intensity operations and the whole higher-level conflict will, in effect, be war.

Operations will still fall into the categories of sea use and sea denial. A generalised strategy seeking 'command of the sea', in the sense envisaged by Mahan, is no longer credible; command will always be challenged by the submarine if nothing else, particularly given an opponent like the Soviet Union which has so many nuclear-powered submarines of great endurance and autonomy. The best that NATO can seek to do is to maintain the use of certain parts of the sea – essentially, moving areas of sea round concentrations of ships whether merchant or military, which may be conducting a variety of tasks from transatlantic reinforcement to air strikes in support of the Supreme Allied Commander Europe. The threat NATO faces is, as we have seen, formidable, and countering it will require large resources.

Against the Soviet surface forces the main vehicles would be nuclear-powered submarines and fixed-wing attack aircraft working from ships or, when range allows, from shore bases. Diverse means of attack, preferably co-ordinated, are perhaps the key to such operations (it is noteworthy that Admiral Gorshkov, the Commander-in-Chief of the Soviet Navy, lays great stress on such methods in his own tactical thinking). This means missiles, suitably varied vehicles, and precise command and control arrangements, well exercised.

Against Soviet air forces, defence in depth is needed: from fighter aircraft, both shore and if possible ship-based, surface-to-air missile systems, and all the tricks of electronic warfare. But even that will not, in the nature of things, be enough and given the long range of Soviet tactical missiles it will be necessary also to be able to shoot down, and spoof, the missiles themselves. These missiles will not, of course, come just from aircraft but from surface ships and submarines too; they pose what is in effect a single air defence problem, but it is a complex and difficult one, demanding very high technology in both sensors and countermeasures in order to defeat it.

The anti-submarine problem is equally severe. Soviet boats are numerous, fast and deep-diving; many are nuclear-powered and missile-armed. Again, defence in depth must be the criterion and all available systems deployed and co-ordinated to the best advantage. Large fixed-wing aircraft using sonobuoys, and nuclear-powered submarines, prefer the 'deep field' away from NATO surface groups; the latter will tend to deploy large helicopters and shipborne systems to fight the battle closer to the piece of sea whose use is being contested.

These higher-level operations are, indeed, the governing case on which the characteristics of the Royal Navy, in its primary NATO role, must be founded. They also, of course, determine the requirements for those shorebased aircraft of the Royal Air Force which fulfil the strike and anti-submarine roles indicated above. Enough has been said here to indicate the diversity of characteristics and technologies that are required; these will be described in more detail in subsequent chapters and a rather more comprehensive description of their use attempted in Chapter XI.

There remains one question which must exercise planners and government alike. Given that a major navy in the NATO alliance must command a wide range of the functions described above, does any navy – apart from that of the USA – require them all? Could not even the Royal Navy specialise in certain roles, relying on the US Navy to fill the rest from the onset of higher level operations?

In the writer's view this is a risk which, in the circumstances, the United Kingdom would be unjustified in taking. The US Navy is severely stretched with worldwide commitments and British maritime forces are expected to take the brunt of operations in the Eastern Atlantic area at the start of hostilities. The ability not only to sustain an attack – from a Soviet Navy whose chief architect puts great emphasis on 'winning the battle for the first salvo' – but to re-enter the conflict and regain the initiative must presuppose large and versatile British forces even in the full NATO context. If one seeks for reassurance in any circumstances where NATO is undecided, or where for any reason United States guarantees are weakened – and heaven forbid that these should occur – then the requirement for a comprehensive Royal Navy is greater and not less.

But there are many other calls on Britain's resources, in the defence field and elsewhere, and no doubt the Royal Navy will continually be called on to exercise all the economies it can sustain. Many will be unpalatable to a Service that has set high standards in both material and training and, often enough, demonstrated their worth operationally. It will aim to maintain, in the face of a set of tasks that – however carefully defined – is diverse, changing and not always predictable, a balanced force that makes the best use of technology, experience and the staying-power that has been the hallmark of the Royal Navy throughout its history.

Below: NATO Exercises: men of the Royal Netherlands Marine Corps embarked in HMS *Hermes* prepare to board their helicopters for a landing. *Crown Copyright*

3

Submarines

There are several good reasons for beginning the more detailed section of this book with a chapter on submarines. First, the proportion of the Royal Navy's resources that goes into submarine procurement, maintenance and running costs increases year by year, and it is already the most submarine-oriented navy in the Western world. Second, submarines are with some justification claimed, and not only by submariners, as the most potent of maritime striking forces. Finally, submarines operate in the sea environment; other units operate half in it or above it; and it is the sea environment that gives sea warfare its unique character.

Below: Launch of a nuclear-powered Fleet submarine at the Vickers Shipbuilders' yard, Barrow-in-Furness. *Crown Copyright*

The Environment

The celebrated truisms about the sea covering 70% of the earth's surface, and about no place on earth being more than 1,720 nautical miles from the sea, are worth repeating. Such a very large body of waters is likely to be complex and imperfectly understood, and it is. A tremendous amount of research has gone into the study of the sea, its characteristics and its resources. The Russians have over 100 oceanographic ships, the Americans not far short of that number; the Royal Navy, with far fewer, did much pioneering work in the field. There is still much to learn, particularly in the remoter areas. But many general facts are (as the Russians say) well known.

The sea is largely impenetrable by waves in the electromagnetic spectrum. This means that both radio (except at very low frequencies indeed) and radar are useless under water. Light, too, finds the sea hard to penetrate, and even in those seas like the Mediterranean where the water is relatively clear, the turbulence of the sea's surface tends to cut down any possibility of observing from above it what is going on underneath.

Sound, on the other hand, travels well under the sea; in the dense water medium the ripple of molecules bumping against each other – which effectively is what sound is – becomes relatively efficient. In consequence, the chief method of sensing under water is by sound, as any porpoise will tell you. Humans call it sonar: passive sonar is essentially listening by hydrophones for the sounds made by underwater vehicles; active sonar is emitting pulses of sound and listening for echoes from underwater vehicles.

But if sound is conducted quite well under water, it is not conducted uniformly. This is because the velocity of sound in the sea varies with temperature, pressure and salinity; these in turn vary with depth and climatic conditions. The consequence is severe bending of sound waves as they pass through variations of sea conditions, resulting in areas or bands of very poor or, conversely, very good sound reception from any particular source. The situation is further complicated by the presence in the sea of vast numbers of independent noise sources, living and non-living: whales, crustacea and fish, turbulence at the sea's surface and bottom. Reflections of sound from the bottom further confuse the situation.

A vehicle, therefore, that is itself very quiet – thus making it intrinsically difficult for a listening 'passive' observer to hear it – and can in addition position itself at the best depth for concealment – thus making its own noise more difficult to hear, and giving the least chance of its echoes returning to any 'active' sound source – is a long way towards escaping aural detection, and in the sea that means invulnerability. It has always been the ambition of the submarine to achieve this desirable state.

Conventional and Nuclear-Powered Submarines

From about 1900 to 1960 the submarine warship was, with rare exceptions, a somewhat hybrid craft that came a long way from the ideal suggested above, because it was not fully independent of the surface. The only way of propelling it under water was by battery-powered electric motors; the batteries needed recharging at frequent intervals; the only way to recharge the batteries was to

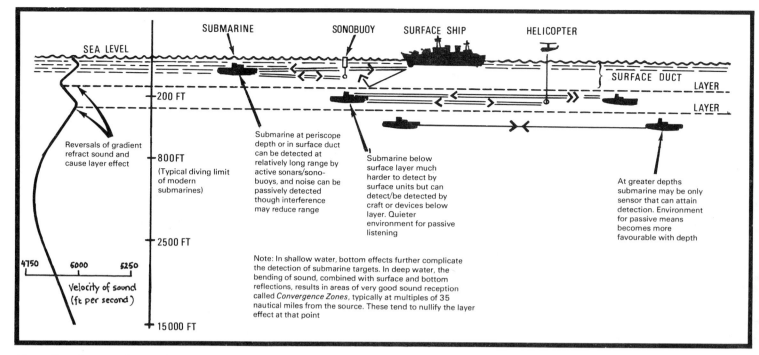

Above: Sound propagation underwater and its effect on submarine detection. *Author*

run the diesel engines; the diesel engines needed air to operate. Even the use of the Snort induction mast, though it allowed the submarine to suck in air while still below the surface, exposed the boat to detection by sensitive aircraft radars and put it in an acoustically bad position in the surface sound duct. The snorting mode was noisy, too.

These difficulties were swept away by the application of nuclear propulsion to the submarine. A nuclear reactor working through a heat exchanger to power a steam turbine formed a closed-cycle system independent of the atmosphere; the system did not, moreover, require refuelling in any conventional sense. The problem of stale air within the submarine, which would otherwise have limited crew endurance, was solved by a combination of devices. An electroyser produced oxygen through the electrolysis of sea water, carbon dioxide scrubbers maintained the level of CO_2 well below the danger level, and further filtration processes kept additional harmful gases, such as carbon monoxide and freon, well in bounds. Nuclear power brought other great benefits: submarine hull form was improved, speed and manoeuvrability were much increased, and the nuclear plant made available ample electrical power to drive sensor, processing and weapon systems as well as domestic services. It is, therefore, quite correct to call the nuclear-powered boat the first true submarine, and to represent it as a quantum jump in underwater and indeed naval warfare. A nuclear-powered submarine is not intrinsically as quiet as a diesel-electric submarine can be on motors, and there are one or two caveats about tactical use which will be discussed later. But there is absolutely no doubt that by embarking early on a programme of nuclear-powered submarines, the Royal Navy kept itself in the front rank of maritime fighting powers: and that rank is a long way ahead of the second.

Patrol Submarines
The Royal Navy, nevertheless, continues to operate a number of diesel-electric submarines of the 'O' class. These represent an advanced, though not the ultimate, development of the 'conventional' boat. Completed between 1960 and 1967, they are 295ft long and have a beam of 26ft. Propulsion on the surface is by Admiralty designed V-16 mechanically supercharged diesel engines, and when submerged by two electric motors supplied by two batteries constructed by Chloride Industrial Batteries, Limited, each of 220 cells (440V DC). Submerged speed is up to

17 knots, but at very high speeds the batteries become exhausted in a matter of hours. Use of low speeds can stretch this to some days.

The pressure hulls of these submarines, in which all the living, machinery, control and weapon spaces are contained, are relatively small in diameter and are surrounded by external ballast tanks which regulate the buoyancy. When the submarine dives, valves are opened which admit sea water to the ballast tanks; positive buoyancy is destroyed and the submarine sinks, aided by the action of hydroplanes which act like the elevators of an aircraft. At the desired depth neutral buoyancy is achieved by adjustment of the amount of water remaining in trimming tanks within the pressure hull, and minor manoeuvres in the vertical plane are carried out by means of the hydroplanes. When the submarine wishes to surface, compressed air is blown into the ballast tanks from sources within the submarine's pressure hull, positive buoyancy is restored and – usually aided by the hydroplanes – the submarine rises to the surface.

The patrol submarine's principal sensor is its passive sonar. If it makes best use of its very low self-noise and ability to manoeuvre at slow underwater speeds, the patrol submarine may expect to have what is called 'sonar advantage' over most other underwater vehicles, particularly when these are bent on other tasks: in transit to an assigned area, moving into position to make an attack on surface units, evading other threats, or returning to base to rearm. All these could entail making more noise than mere lurking would do. The patrol submarine will, of course, be able to detect surface craft before they detect it. Passive sonar can provide the patrol submarine with directional information, and the noise received will often provide enough special characteristics to permit classification of the target. Passive ranging is a more difficult problem. Active sonar provides a point of reference on the transmission of a 'ping', and measurement of the time an echo takes to return gives the range. Passive sonar provides no such reference. There are ways of integrating the rate of change of bearing with estimates of speed and course in order to find the range, and some lateral spacing of hydrophones with the consequent chance of correlation may offer further possibilities, but by and large passive ranging is uncertain. Active sonar, if used even in a short burst, is likely to find the range on a target that is close enough; but it also announces the presence of the patrol submarine, so tends to be used with caution.

The other sensors available to the patrol submarine operate across the sea-air interface, that is to say they must be used at periscope depth or above. There are two periscopes, for search and for attack, the latter particularly slim and precise. There is a search receiver which can give warning of aircraft or ships in the submarine's vicinity – provided they are transmitting on radar. Finally, the submarine itself has a high-definition radar which

Above: HMS *Osiris*, **a conventionally-powered patrol submarine, leaves Faslane. The buildings of HMS** *Neptune* **and the naval base are in the background.** *Crown Copyright*

Left: In the engine room of the patrol submarine *Ocelot.* *Crown Copyright*

33

Above: A patrol submarine passes the Royal Naval College, Greenwich, on a visit to London. *Crown Copyright*

Right: In the control room of the patrol submarine *Odin*. *Crown Copyright*

Below right: Living conditions are cramped but crews are cheerful: bunks in the 'fore ends' (torpedo space) of HMS *Odin*. *Crown Copyright*

Above: HMS *Dreadnought*, the first nuclear-powered fleet submarine in the Royal Navy. Photograph by Leading Airman Eric Rooke.
Crown Copyright

will detect surface targets at relatively short range. All these above-water sensors entail putting something up above the surface and thereby exposing the submarine to radar detection; use of the radar, in addition, risks its detection by the search receivers of enemy surface or aircraft. Moreover, periscope depth is usually the least satisfactory depth for hiding from surface ship and helicopter sonars, since it is in the surface duct. But in order to conduct a precise, close range attack on surface craft a submarine – however powered – generally needs to take such risks.

The main weapon of the patrol submarine is still the torpedo; the 'O' Class have six bow and two stern tubes with stowage for twenty and four torpedoes respectively. For attack against other submarines they are now provided with a much more sophisticated weapon than the time-honoured (and very reliable) Mark 8** with which Lieutenant-Commander James Launders, in 1945, conducted the very first submerged submarine-versus-submarine attack. The new weapon, the Tigerfish, manufactured by Marconi Space and Defence Systems, is a homing weapon, wire-guided from the submarine in the initial stages of its approach but independently completing the attack with the help of its own sonar. The range and speed of the torpedo have not been announced, but it is worth noting that the torpedo is claimed to be particularly quiet. Given this characteristic, against an unalerted target speed does not matter much.

For attacking surface ships the Tigerfish is, of course, available if the conditions are right; but so is a straight-running, straightforward, fast, reliable torpedo called, oddly, the Mark 8**. It is probably the longest-serving weapon in the Royal Navy; but so long as there are still situations where it is an adequate weapon, there is no urgent call to discard it. Those situations – for example, attacking surface units whose anti-submarine capability is limited, or counter-attacking hunting surface units – do still occur. Torpedoes are, notably, weapons that sink ships; missiles may only disable them.

One more humdrum peacetime task of patrol submarines should be mentioned: this is providing submarine targets for the sea training of anti-submarine forces. The more basic this training is, the more the submarine's role is that of a 'clockwork mouse'; advanced exercises give the submariners, too, scope for their skills.

Life on board a patrol submarine in the 1980s is not at all unlike submarine life in the preceding 60 years. Conditions are cramped, facilities for washing are limited, food tends to become monotonous after a few days at sea. With a crew of seven Officers and 62 Ratings, a patrol submarine needs a very high degree of knowledge and dedication in every single member. The great majority will be volunteers for the Submarine Service, and all will have attended a specialist training school for six weeks followed by three months at sea. Then, if he passes the examination, a man becomes a qualified submariner and is entitled to wear the

submarine badge. The expertise and responsibility that everyone on board a submarine must and does show breeds mutual trust that is at once apparent in the relaxed, informal yet totally disciplined atmosphere that exists throughout the boat. Probably it is a bit more apparent in the patrol submarines than their nuclear cousins; the cheek-by-jowl existence, the spartan conditions and the looming presence of the job in every valve, handle and gauge all over the boat, all encourage a slightly piratical team spirit and scotch any pomposity.

Naturally when they can get into better accommodation, submariners do. When the boat is in harbour for any length of time, officers and ratings live ashore. The bases at HMS *Dolphin* (Gosport), *Neptune* (Faslane), and *Drake* (Devonport) can all be used for this purpose. Depot ships, which used to take their stately bulk round the oceans and gather submarines round them when in harbour, no longer operate, but now that even patrol submarines are so much more mobile and self-sufficient, and the Royal Navy is more concentrated in the NATO area than it used to be, their absence is not a serious drawback.

Fleet Submarines
At the time of publication of this book the Royal Navy has 13 nuclear-powered Fleet submarines in service, and three more are building. The interval between launches has historically been about 15 months, and the life of a submarine can be estimated as something between 20 and 25 years.

Though there has been a steady evolutionary improvement in design, to the extent that five different classes of Fleet submarine are identified in the table at the end of the book, the basic characteristics of the all-British boats (the first of all, HMS *Dreadnought*, had a US-supplied power plant) are similar. They are about 280ft long, with a beam of 33ft. This gives a very different hull-form from that of a patrol submarine; the peardrop shape of the Fleet submarine is very efficient under water, both for speed and manoeuvrability. Ballast tanks are internal, which means that the pressure hull makes up the whole girth of the boat and is thus very roomy. Displacement is 3,500 tons on the surface and 4,500 tons submerged.

Sensor systems, benefitting from the abundant electrical supplies that are an important by-product of nuclear power, can be very powerful. Though this is particularly applicable to active sonar, and as we have seen there are tactical problems attending too free a use of this means of detection, it also allows the most

Above: Very like a whale: the pear-shaped hull form of HMS *Valiant* is rather cumbersome on the surface but very efficient when dived.
Crown Copyright

sophisticated processing of the input from passive hydrophone arrays and the potential to make maximum use of any further development in passive sonar.

Available weapon systems for some years lagged behind the potential of Fleet submarines as offensive units. Now, however, the introduction of Tigerfish and its up-to-date modifications – making the homing head even more sensitive and difficult to spoof – and of the Harpoon anti-ship missile has given the Fleet submarine an adequate armoury.

The Harpoon is an American weapon. It is fired from a torpedo tube, so its diameter is 21ins; it is 15ft 5ins long and weighs about 1500lb. On firing (by compressed air, as are torpedoes) it ascends to the surface, its rocket motor ignites, its stub wings unfold, and it sets off on a preset course towards its target. Its homing head is activated on approaching the target area and on detecting the target it homes in and strikes with a conventional warhead of considerable explosive power. The whole flight path is at a very low altitude above sea level, giving the minimum chance of the target's detecting the incoming missile by radar. In early 1980 it was reported that HMS *Churchill* had completed the Royal Navy's proving trials of Harpoon: all six missiles fired had scored hits.

The Harpoon's maximum range is reported as 60 miles. This raises some interesting questions, for that range is a long way outside any precise target location that could be achieved in normal circumstances by the submarine's own sensors. Either the submarine must be told, through the sea-air interface by some aircraft or ship above it, just where the target is; or it must fire on directional information only, 'into the brown' as submariners say; or it must wait for more precise information as the range closes. These are real problems, and much thought – or perhaps, some improvements in sensing methods – will be needed to get the best solution, but it is better to have a missile that sets problems than to have no missile.

In microcosm, the whole question of integrating a Fleet submarine's activities with those of the Fleet is given above. No submariner would pretend that, when below periscope depth, his sensors give him a complete picture of the tactical situation round him. Most obviously, he has no means of knowing what aircraft are present above his immediate area, but there are other uncertainties about the presence of opposing passive sensors – particularly sonobuoys – and the precise location and identity of surface ships. The only way he can get a comprehensive picture is to listen to reports from friendly units the other side of the interface; but such communication is not intrinsically easy, though advances are being made in underwater telephony from link ships and radio communication via submarine-trailed aerials. If it is desired to use a submarine in the tactical support of the Fleet, whether against surface or subsurface threats, to the best advantage all these problems have to be thought through and their solutions exercised. This of course goes on, in the Maritime Tactical School and at sea, and the Royal Navy is probably as far ahead as any – the Soviet and US Navies not excepted – in realising Lord Fisher's dream of making full use of the submarine's potential as a Fleet unit.

When all is said and done, most people in Fleet submarines probably prefer a more independent life away from the immediate vicinity of friendly surface units, stalking their prey whether submarine or surface ship, untrammelled by any doubt as to its enemy character. They are of course well suited to such excursions into waters infested by hostile forces. How much of their operations can take place there will depend on the strategic situation.

Enough has been said here, perhaps, to indicate that in the writer's view phrases like 'the capital ship of the future' are a thought too glib as descriptions of the Fleet submarine, and that the thesis that 'the Navy must go under water' is altogether too simple. The Fleet submarine is an offensive weapons system of great power and survivability, and it is an ideal unit for exercising sea denial, but if it attempts to control the surface it is acting out of character and temporarily loses all its advantages. Seeing that there is no prospect of cargoes going beneath the surface, that limitation is an important one. But the Fleet submarine is probably the unit of the Royal Navy, above all others, that gives Soviet tacticians and planners the most problems.

Life in a Fleet submarine is more comfortable than in a patrol boat. The submarine is at depth for days, often weeks, on end and this enables everyone to settle into a steady watchkeeping routine except, of course, when an exercise or operation moves into an intensive phase. Accommodation, though not spacious, is adequate to give every man a part of the boat that is 'his' corner. There is plenty of fresh water, distilled from sea water by the

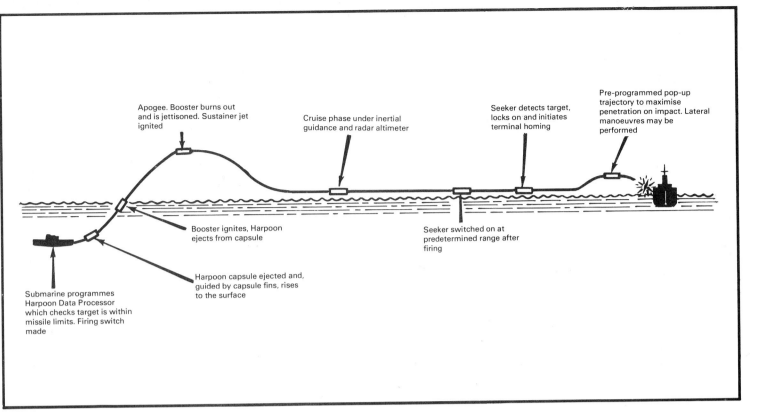

Apogee. Booster burns out and is jettisoned. Sustainer jet ignited

Cruise phase under inertial guidance and radar altimeter

Seeker detects target, locks on and initiates terminal homing

Pre-programmed pop-up trajectory to maximise penetration on impact. Lateral manoeuvres may be performed

Booster ignites, Harpoon ejects from capsule

Seeker switched on at predetermined range after firing

Harpoon capsule ejected and, guided by capsule fins, rises to the surface

Submarine programmes Harpoon Data Processor which checks target is within missile limits. Firing switch made

Above: Harpoon operational sequence. *Author*

Left: **On board the fleet submarine** *Warspite*, **the foreplanesman controls the attitude of the submarine in the vertical plane.**
Crown Copyright

Below left: **The nuclear-powered fleet submarine** *Sovereign* **at the North Pole, October 1976. After 10 days under the icecap, conducting geophysical survey work, the submarine surfaced through a polynya – a patch of relatively thin ice.**
Crown Copyright

evaporator system, and the food is both excellent and varied since refrigeration and cooking are no problem (though certain cooking fats, being incompatible with the air purification plant, are forbidden). There is a well-stocked library, films are plentiful and static recreation – rowing machines and get-nowhere bicycles – is provided.

Fleet submarines are a commander's command; the commanding officer will have been in charge of a patrol submarine at an earlier stage of his career and have done a nuclear course, as will all his officers and – to differing levels of 'need to know' – his crew. However many interlocks and fail-safe devices there may be – and nuclear-powered submarines are superbly well equipped with these – it is always the men, and their attitude of mind as well as their state of training, who are the most important safety factors as well as the boat's operators in action conditions.

Polaris Submarines

The British Polaris project, following on the Nassau Agreement of 1962 which led to the Royal Navy's being charged with the custody and, if necessary, delivery of Britain's strategic nuclear deterrent, is one of the most startling examples of swift and ordered technical development and production in our history. The bare facts are that in just under seven years, four very large (7,000 ton) nuclear-powered submarines were designed, built, equipped with ballistic missiles, and completed so that since 1969 there has never been a moment when the Polaris force did not have at least one submarine on patrol. An operating base and full shore support facilities were built concurrently. Even though the missiles themselves were supplied by the United States and US help was unstinted, it was a notable achievement.

The Polaris submarines share many characteristics with the Fleet boats: their power plants, ancillary systems and many of their sensor systems are common. The armament is, however, quite different. The whole midship section is taken up with 16 vertical tubes each housing a Polaris missile. These are 31 feet long, solid-fuelled, two-stage ballistic missiles with a range of the order of 2,500 nautical miles. Each carries multiple nuclear warheads, British designed and built. These are not independently targetted: that is, all warheads from one missile will strike the same target. This, it appears, will still be the case

Below: Fleet submarines have visited many foreign countries and made round-the-world deployments. Extensive safety measures and excellent crew training ensure that there is no pollution hazard. *Crown Copyright*

Above: The ballistic missile submarine *Repulse* at Plymouth. *Crown Copyright*

Left: The integrated monitoring panel in the missile compartment of the nuclear powered Polaris submarine HMS *Resolution*.
Crown Copyright

when the new British front end, codenamed Chevaline, comes into service in the early 1980s. This system is designed to counter improved Soviet anti-ballistic missile measures, and can be expected to include ways of physically protecting the warheads against anti-ballistic missile blast as well as presenting the Soviet early warning radars with a very large number of widely-separated decoy targets in space, thus ensuring that if ever the Polaris has to be fired, enough warheads will get through to inflict on the Soviet Union damage which it would find unacceptable.

Control of such a very formidable system — each submarine has a firepower greater than all the bombs dropped by both sides in World War II – is, naturally, a matter of great moment and concern. It is, first, entirely national. British ministers have categorically denied the suggestion, which surfaces from time to time, that there is some form of American veto over the use of Polaris. Second, the decision to fire would of course be entirely in political hands. The primary means of transmitting it would be by very low frequency radio, the only sort that can be heard by a submarine at depth. Back-up means of transmission exist but are a closely guarded secret. Once a firing message is received on board a Polaris submarine, it must be independently authenticated to the captain by two officers using entirely different authentication data. The firing procedure is complex but, because it is computer-aided, swift. The boat's position is constantly fed into the fire-control computers by the highly accurate Ship's Inertial Navigation System (SINS – yet another system shared with the Fleet submarines). From this, and given the preset target co-ordinates, the computers calculate guidance requirements and cross-check them. Missile launch is by high-pressure gas; on surfacing, the missile motor ignites. First-stage separation and second-stage ignition occur after about one minute, and the inertial guidance system with extremely precise gyroscopes, accelerometers and digital computer puts the missile on course, correcting yaw, pitch and roll. At a predetermined moment the guidance system shuts off the rocket motors and triggers separation of the re-entry bodies from the rest of the missile. They would then follow a ballistic trajectory to the target. On the advent of Chevaline, which is stated to include the ability to manoeuvre the payload in space, this final phase could be expected to include the dispensing of penetration aids: decoys with a radar signature very similar to that of the warheads themselves.

The ability to go through that sequence, at any moment of a patrol lasting 60 days or so, is the Polaris submarine's whole reason for being. It is not in the business of seeking out opposing tactical units; indeed, if it detects any it is its business to 'lose' them. Equipped as it is with very good passive sensors, capable of high speed and manoeuvrability, and helped by the most advanced submarine quietening measures, it is well able to do this. There is a world of difference in the detectability of a submarine that is being operated to avoid detection and that of a submarine being used tactically. The Polaris submarines do have six tubes for conventional homing torpedoes, but these are self-defence weapons to be used only as a last resort if by any chance the submarine is detected and comes under attack in wartime.

All the amenities of a Fleet submarine are available also to the crew of a Polaris boat. The food is, indeed, generally even better, and the films tend to be more modern. Each crew member can receive news from home once a week, by what is called a familygram; much ingenuity goes into fitting into 40 words all that needs to be said, particularly as there is no possibility of supplementary questions from the boat, which of course keeps strict radio silence throughout its patrol.

To get maximum utilisation of the Polaris submarines, each has two crews which man her for alternate patrols; the off-duty crew are ashore at the Faslane base undergoing refresher training, taking leave, breaking in new crew members, spending some time with their families and in general preparing to go back to sea. Each crew has 13 Officers and 130 Ratings, with a commander in command and a lieutenant-commander as executive officer. Both will have successful previous commands of submarines in their records, and like all the rest of the officers will have done a variety of courses at Faslane, Greenwich and, for the engineers, Gosport or Dounreay, to fit them for duty in a ballistic missile submarine. The proportion of senior rates to juniors is unusually high,

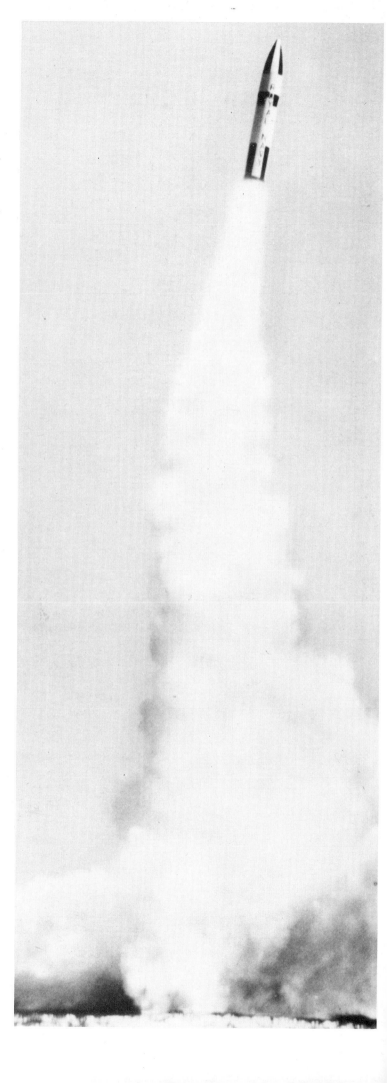

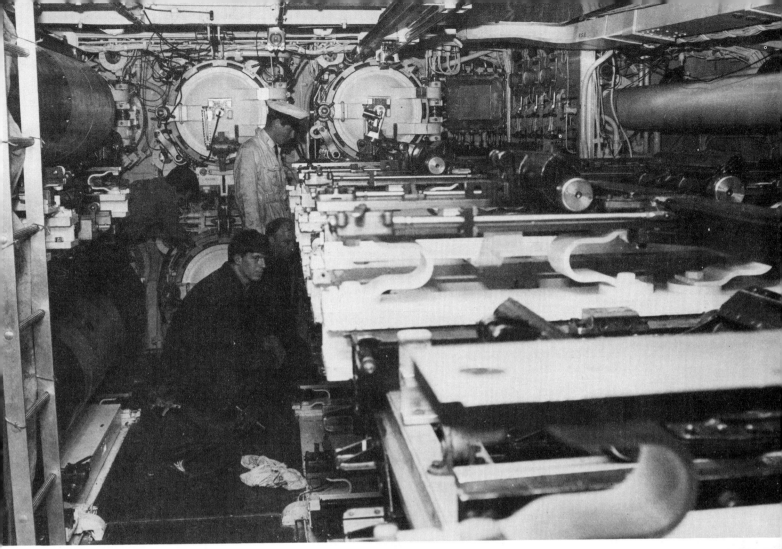

Left: A British Polaris missile on a test firing from the Cape Canaveral range. *Crown Copyright*

Above: The torpedo tube space on board HMS *Resolution*. Compare this with the tube space in HMS *Odin*, page 34. *Crown Copyright*

Right: In the galley on board HMS *Resolution*. *Crown Copyright*

perhaps due to the need not only for technical experience but for a certain gravitas. Life on board a Polaris submarine is cheerful enough, but less than any other in the naval service is it a frivolous job.

Deterrence is not an easy concept to hoist in, depending as it does on the manifest ability to do terrible damage in order that no one else should be tempted to do similar things to one's own country. Mere possession of the potential is not enough: it must be ready, certain, and sufficient. Inevitably, therefore, the crew of a Polaris submarine will concentrate on ensuring that if the deterrent is ever used, it will be entirely effective. Yet they will know that if use is ever ordered, the deterrent will have failed to deter. The fact that for 35 years there has been no major conflict, and that this must in large part be due to the balance of nuclear deterrence, and that this in turn must owe a good deal to the extra complexities introduced by the British independent contribution to Western deterrence, must be important incentives to their dedication to their vastly responsible task.

Submarines: The Future
The proportion of the Navy's resources spent on submarines will continue to rise. While submarines have limitations, particularly in low-intensity operations and as sea control vehicles, their capacity to pose a continuous overt or covert threat, their offensive power and relative invulnerability are such that they offer vast potential dividends. But funds for submarine construction and improvement will be limited, and nuclear-powered boats are very expensive; they are quoted in the 1981 Defence White Paper at £175 million each. Consequently they will be supplemented by a new class of patrol submarines. These will make use of many lessons learnt in Fleet boats as well as the 'O' class – they will be tubbier, perhaps single-screw, with particularly advanced passive sonars. They will not be merely coastal or training submarines; it is very much against naval thinking to produce a lot of vessels that have a dubious role in war.

Improvements in Fleet submarines will to be sought mainly to maintain the all-important sonar advantage both by further quietening and by improved passive detection equipment, including towed arrays which are reported to give the prospect of significantly improved sensitivity and, ultimately, precision. Communications with both surface ships and aircraft will need further improvement if the Fleet submarine is to become a regular fully-integrated unit of the Fleet; on the other hand, new concepts of sea control operations may allow Fleet submarines a more autonomous yet fully contributory role. The prospect is an exciting one, involving constant thought and experiment on how to use this great and still evolving potential.

Finally, the Government has announced its decision to replace the Polaris submarines, during the 1990s, with a force of ballistic missile submarines armed with the American Trident missile system, which was chosen from a number of possible options after a great deal of careful study. This system, with a range of about 4,500 nautical miles, can deliver up to eight independently-targetted warheads (MIRVs) per missile. The warheads will, as in Polaris, be British designed and built. So, of course, will the submarines. This development offers enough robustness against changes in opposing anti-ballistic and anti-submarine capabilities to ensure the continuance of the independent British strategic nuclear deterrent well into the 21st century.

Right: Accurate navigation is a prerequisite for effective ballistic missile firing and hence deterrence. HMS *Repulse* is in coastal waters here, as can be seen from the chart, but the same accuracy is available in the open ocean with modern aids. *Crown Copyright*

4

The Surface Fleet

Previous chapters of this book have shown that in many aspects of sea operations surface ships must still bear the main burden. This is particularly true of low-intensity operations; but it has not been Admiralty Board policy to design ships specifically for such tasks. The need to deter, and to make a full contribution to NATO's maritime combat forces, means that the ability to fight in operations at the higher level is a prime consideration in designing the ships of the surface fleet.

Surface ships can, of course, do certain things particularly well at any level of warfare, and they can do some things that no other system, air or subsurface, can do at all.

First, they are able to acquire, collate, process and disseminate very large amounts of information, and to transmit the orders necessary for the most effective application of available forces to the task in hand. Second, they can provide air defence, by shipboard systems, against aircraft and missiles both for themselves and for other ships in close proximity. Third, they can deploy aircraft, both fixed and rotary-wing, in strike, air defence and anti-submarine roles, from their own decks without regard to distance from bases ashore. Fourth, they are a prerequisite for amphibious operations.

Surface ships can do these things principally because they are large, densely populated, highly mechanised dwellers on the dividing line between sea and sky; and it is no accident that man, with the great bulk of his across-the-sea transport, lives on that interface too. But these very qualities make the surface ship vulnerable to attack both from the air and under the sea, and thus a proportion of its weapon systems must necessarily be provided to enhance its prospects of survival. If, however, the proportion of self-defence systems is so high that scarcely anything is left over to take the offensive, the ship is not much use; and, given the number of options now presented by modern techniques for weapons and sensors in the above-water environment, striking the right balance is a problem for planners and designers.

The Above-Water Environment

While almost as complex as the sea beneath it, the earth's atmosphere is rather less baffling as an environment in which to fight. The chief aberrations are caused by weather conditions and are, generally, of less severe and lasting effect than those under the surface – provided, of course, that the technology and expertise exist to overcome them.

Electromagnetic waves travel well in the atmosphere. Because they go at the speed of light and because variations in them are very quickly and precisely detectable by modern electronics, extremely large quantities of data can be transmitted, received and exchanged. The main limitation is that most electromagnetic waves will only travel in a straight-line path, except in unusual and unpredictable conditions; therefore they are, effectively, horizon-limited. The well-known exception is in the high-frequency band (3-30kHz), where waves bounce off the ionosphere and so skip round the world, is useful to ships for communications only.

As in the subsurface environment, sensors can be active or passive. Radar, the chief active sensor, operates basically by emitting very short pulses of radio energy at frequencies of 200kHz upwards, and receiving and processing the energy reflected by air or surface targets. Bearing is given by the direction in which the aerial is pointing, range by measuring the time the pulse takes to go out and return. Radar performance can be degraded by sea, cloud and rain returns, and much of the complexity of modern equipment stems from the need to minimise these effects. Radar can also be jammed by electronic emitters working on its frequency, and modern equipments incorporate measures such as rapid random frequency shifts to counter these; the techniques fall under the headings of Electronic Countermeasures (ECM) and Electronic Counter-countermeasures (ECCM), respectively, in the jargon of electronic warfare.

Electronic emissions, either on radio or radar frequencies, are detectable by search receivers and direction-finding gear, and it is in the nature of the active-passive equation that a radar emission

Below: HMS *Glamorgan*, flying a Rear-Admiral's flag, leads a Royal Navy Task Group out of Portsmouth at the start of a round-the-world deployment. Radar aerials to be seen include gunnery control, above the bridge; target indication, at the top of the foremast; air warning, on the mainmast. Communication aerials include the vertical whips, and the ultra high frequency (UHF) cones at the yardarms. *Crown Copyright*

can nearly always be detected before it can get an echo from its detector. This does not necessarily matter if the detector cannot hide; but he is at least warned. Such measures are called Electronic Support Measures (ESM); with ECM and ECCM they go to make up the complex electronic warfare scene.

Miniaturisation of components has meant that electronic emitters and receivers can now be contained in very small packages, and this has led to their incorporation in air-breathing tactical missiles. Micro-circuitry has allowed programming of missiles to the extent that after launch they can be autonomous. A missile will, of course, only be as good as its programming and the target settings that are fed into it. The techniques available include homing passively on a target radar, and on heat-sources by infra-red detection, as well as homing on echoes from a target found by an active radar seeker on board the missile. Very low altitudes can be achieved by the use of radar altimeters and evasive manoeuvres can be built in.

The Soviet Union has not been slow to exploit all the possibilities presented by advancing technology in the above-water environment, and their forces present a progressively more severe threat of which full account must be taken in the Royal Navy's surface ship programme.

A Rolling Programme

The programme of design and construction has been, broadly speaking, continuous and evolutionary. This is not to say that considerable shifts have not occurred, the most notable being the reappraisal and recasting caused by the cancellation in the mid-1960s of a new generation of strike aircraft carriers. But these have been waves and eddies in a pretty steady stream, whose direction and continuity have been much influenced by the permanent Royal Corps of Naval Constructors and by a national programme of weapon development. There is both consistency and commonality of weapons systems among the various classes of ship now in service: in their descriptions below, a weapon system will be covered in detail only once, under the class of ship of which it is a salient characteristic.

Aircraft Carriers

It is with no sense of nostalgia that a discussion of aircraft carrier starts with the old *Ark Royal*, now in the breakers' yard. This, the last of the fixed-wing strike carriers in the Royal Navy, displaced 45,000 tons and could carry a squadron of anti-submarine helicopters as well as two squadrons of high-performance fixed wing aircraft for striking surface targets and for air defence. She was an all-role ship, as self-sufficient as a single ship of that size could be. When it was decided that no comparable successor should be built, responsibility for the long-range air defence of the Fleet – that is, the interception of enemy aircraft before they can launch their missiles – passed to the Royal Air Force, as did that for long-range air strikes on enemy surface units. This task lies with Strike Command aircraft operating mainly from bases in Scotland.

Nevertheless there was still a need to deploy, in numbers, the highly capable anti-submarine helicopters, to provide air defence and to exercise command of complex and diverse maritime forces in ocean areas, in order to ensure use of the sea: the prime NATO maritime task. On analysis it emerged that the most cost-effective way of doing these things was to co-locate them in a unit of 15-20,000 tons displacement, and thus the *Invincible* class, originally called the 'through-deck cruiser', was conceived. Unsurprisingly for a vessel designed to operate numbers of aircraft, her chief external feature was a flat top. This, and an all-gas turbine power plant, were firm components of the design from an early stage, as was a Sea Dart air defence missile system. The most important later addition was the incorporation of arrangements to operate Vertical/Short Take-off and Landing

Below: HMS *Invincible*, **the first of the Navy's new generation of aircraft carriers, on trials. Her normal complement will include anti-submarine helicopters and V/STOL fixed wing aircraft.** *Crown Copyright*

(V/STOL) fixed-wing aircraft. These would provide the ship with the ability to deny the airspace round it to enemy reconnaissance, to probe over the horizon for threats, and to threaten strikes against opposing surface units – all at short notice and independently of shore resources.

HMS *Invincible*, the name ship of the class, was launched by Her Majesty the Queen at the Barrow-in-Furness yard of Vickers Shipbuilders Limited on 3 May 1977. She commissioned in June 1980. Her sister ships, *Illustrious* and *Ark Royal*, are being built by Swan Hunter at Wallsend-on-Tyne.

The ship is of 16,000 tons standard displacement, is 677ft (206m) long overall and has a maximum beam of 105ft (32m). She is powered by four Rolls-Royce Olympus TM3B gas turbines rated at 20,880kW each. These drive into two David Brown triple-reduction reversing gearboxes and thence to two fixed-pitch propellers. Elaborate cross-feeding arrangements ensure maximum flexibility in case of damage. Electrical power is supplied by eight Paxman Valenta 1,175mW generators; these are in no less than six different machinery spaces so, again, action damage is well catered for. Fresh water is supplied by five Stone Platt auxiliary boilers. The whole machinery plant is monitored by the Decca ISIS system in the machinery control room.

The ship's command, control and information system is designed to make the maximum use of all the information sources available, both internal and external. The operations room system is called ADAWS (Action Data and Weapons System) Type 6, and includes Ferranti FM 1600 computers and Plessey displays for information and fire control. Communications are provided by the proven, but very advanced and flexible, Marconi ICS 3 system giving ample transmission and reception facilities in all usable communication bands. Satellite communication terminals are provided. The ship's own sensors include Type 1022 air warning radar, incorporating Hollandse-Signaal transmitting and receiving equipment and a Marconi aerial; Type 992 Q for target indication; Type 909 for Sea Dart control and Type 1006 for navigation. Electronic warfare equipment is clearly carried but details have not been published. There is a ship-

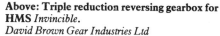

Above: Triple reduction reversing gearbox for HMS *Invincible*.
David Brown Gear Industries Ltd

Left: In the hangar, HMS *Invincible*.
Crown Copyright

Above: HMS *Hermes*, **an aircraft carrier of an earlier generation but capable of carrying an aircraft complement similar to** *Invincible's*. *Crown Copyright*

Left: HMS *Hermes* **taking part in a NATO exercise in her commando carrier role.** *Crown Copyright*

mounted sonar, though of course the ship's anti-submarine reach is given by the embarked helicopters.

The aircraft complement consists of nine Westland Sea King Mark 2 anti-submarine helicopters and five Hawker Siddeley Sea Harrier V/STOL aircraft. All can be stowed below in the hangar and a full range of stores and servicing equipment is carried. To enable the Harrier to take off with the best possible payload, a 'ski-jump' with a 7° up-angle is provided at the forward end of the flight deck. The flight deck itself is angled at 6° from the fore and aft line to facilitate aircraft operations and keep the forward arc of fire clear for Sea Dart.

Invincible is a good ship to live in. Accommodation standards are high and facilities extensive: there are dining halls, recreation spaces and an extensive library, all separate from the sleeping areas. The ship's company of 131 officers, 265 senior ratings and 604 junior ratings represent a great variety of specialisations and skills, reinforced when the squadrons are on board.

But the *Invincible* is, most definitely, a fighting ship. There is a great deal of built-in toughness in protection against nuclear and chemical contamination, in damage control and watertight integrity, as well as offensive and sea control capability; she is not a ship that any opponent could brush aside, and could be ignored only at his peril. And, of course, her reach extends far beyond herself, not only in her aircraft but in her capacity for command and control.

No one could deny that the *Invincible* class has been long in gestation. In consequence – and after several shifts of the wind of change – one older aircraft carrier remains in commission with a dual role as an anti-submarine and amphibious Ship. This is HMS *Hermes*. She spent much of her life as a fixed-wing carrier and consequently has an angled deck, comprehensive action information facilities and air warning radar of reasonable range.

During her last refit, completed in 1981, she was given a 7° ski-jump which will enable her to operate Sea Harriers, and her standard aircraft complement will now be 12 Sea Kings and five Sea Harriers. She will however continue to have a secondary role as an amphibious ship, carrying in this role a Royal Marines Commando Group of about 750 men operating RN Sea King and Wessex 5 helicopters as well as Royal Marines Lynx and Gazelle. To do this she would, of course, have to disembark most of her anti-submarine Sea Kings and the Sea Harrier squadron.

Of some 24,000 tons and with steam turbines of 76,000 shaft horse power, she has a basic complement of 980, with additions according to her current role and the air squadrons and Royal Marines embarked in consequence. She is a big ship in every sense of the term – the biggest in the Royal Navy, in fact, since she is some 70ft longer than *Invincible* – and, though not in her first youth, demonstrates the adaptability and scope of surface ships. Certainly NATO, and particularly our Norwegian allies, would feel less secure if this important unit was not available.

Destroyers
The evolutionary and logical nature of medium-sized surface-ship development has scarcely extended to nomenclature. Ever since it reintroduced the term 'frigate' at the latter end of World War II, but retained the word 'destroyer', the Royal Navy has teetered on the brink of absurdity in seeking to distinguish between the two, particularly as both sorts of ships became progressively larger and frequently leapfrogged in size. However, by and large it can be said that destroyers have a primary air defence role, while frigates have a primary anti-submarine role.

The County *Class*
The first generation of ships designed primarily to deploy air defence missile systems was a class of eight 5,440ton vessels named after British counties, of which five remained in service in mid-1981. They came into commission between 1963 and 1970. They are, by common consent, some of the handsomest warships ever built, with superb lines tapering towards the stern and very well-proportioned superstructure and funnels. Bigger than many inter-war cruisers, they are powered by a composite plant of two steam and four gas turbines. Gas turbine boost allows a quick getaway but, in this system, there are complexities which are reflected in the large engineroom complements of these ships. The total ship's company is 485.

Above: A County Class guided missile destroyer. Prominent features include, from left, the Sea Slug launcher, Wessex 3 Helicopter, Type 901 guidance radar, Type 277 heightfinding and Type 965M air warning radar. *Crown Copyright*

Left: Sea Slug drill on board a County class guided missile destroyer. With restricted deckhead space in the magazine, hard hats are compulsory headgear. *Crown Copyright*

Right: HMS *Fife* at speed. The Exocet canisters, replacing 'B' turret just before the bridge, can be clearly seen. Photo by Leading Airman Ian Ferguson. *Crown Copyright*

The most characteristic, and probably the most important, item of the armament is the Sea Slug missile. This is a first-generation system in which the missile 'rides' to its aircraft target up a beam designated by the associated Type 901 radar. The Sea Slug Mark 2, fitted in *Antrim, Glamorgan, Fife* and *Norfolk*, can in addition engage surface targets. The system is all-weather, though probably somewhat susceptible to the effects of clutter from sea and weather returns. The Sea Slug launcher – fortunately for the look of the ship – is mounted on the quarterdeck.

Originally, the County Class mounted four 4.5 inch guns in twin mountings forward. In later ships of the class 'B' mounting has now been replaced by four Aerospatiale Exocet MM38 surface-to-surface missiles. With a maximum effective range of 38 kilometres (20.7 nautical miles) these do much to redress the imbalance of range between Western surface ships and missile-armed surface craft of other navies. The missile, 17ft (5.2m) long and weighing 1,617lb (735kg), is contained in a sealed canister, requiring only user checks when on board. Before firing, it is fed with a designated target position. After launch, during which the launcher must point within 30° of the target's bearing, the missile settles under inertial guidance on a course which will bring it to the target area. It flies at a sea-skimming altitude under the influence of a radar altimeter. At a given distance from the target position, its active radar seeker is switched on and on detecting the target it homes in by a proportional navigation system, delivering a 352lb (160kg) high explosive warhead. Very good resistance to electronic countermeasures, and a 93% success rate in practice firings, are claimed by the makers. Exocet is also fitted in several of the frigate class described later in this chapter.

The County Class also carry two quadruple Sea Cat mountings for close-in air defence; a Wessex 3 anti-submarine helicopter; and a variety of sensors including a Type 184 panoramic medium-range sonar, a Type 965 air warning radar, Type 992 Q target indication radar and Type 978 heightfinding radar. They have therefore a good deal of versatility, and have frequently acted as flagships of group deployments around the world.

HMS Bristol

The class of which HMS *Bristol* was the first and only representative – the Type 82 – was designed to act as an air defence escort of the new generation of fixed-wing carriers, and died with it. The completion of *Bristol*, however, was valuable in providing a platform for trials of the new Sea Dart and Ikara missile systems, and the ship herself is a most useful command and control unit, incorporating as she does much modern sensor processing and communications equipment. She is unusual in two respects: she is the only three-funnelled ship in the Royal Navy, and she has no helicopter hangar.

The Sheffield Class

This class, also called the Type 42, is already the most numerous surface ship type in the Royal Navy apart from the *Leander* frigates. The programme began with HMS *Sheffield*, launched in 1971. The ships were designed to provide most of the capabilities of the *Bristol* on a much smaller hull and with two-thirds of the complement.

The first ten ships of the class have a standard displacement of 3,500 tons and a length of 410ft (125m). HMS *Manchester* and subsequent ships will be 300 tons heavier and 40ft longer. The power plant is all gas turbine. It consists of two Rolls-Royce Olympus, rated at 20,000kW each, for high-speed running and

Above: A new generation in Operations Rooms: HMS *Bristol*. *Crown Copyright*

Right: HMS *Sheffield*, name ship of the Type 42 destroyer class. All gas turbine powered and armed with Sea Dart missiles, a 4.5 inch gun and Lynx helicopter, these effective ships form one of the Royal Navy's most numerous surface ship classes. *Crown Copyright*

Below right: A Lynx helicopter prepares to land on board HMS *Birmingham*, a destroyer of the Sheffield class. Photo by Petty Officer Les Warr. *Crown Copyright*

two Rolls-Royce Tyne for cruising. They work through gearboxes to two Stone Manganese controllable-pitch propellers. With this arrangement excellent acceleration can be combined with fuel economy. Gas turbines inevitably mean large air downtakes and access patches for quick removal of machinery, since it is easier to repair by replacement than to do something in situ. These facilities are provided. Electrical power is supplied by four diesel generators in two separate auxiliary machinery spaces. Redundancy and stoutness are notable damage control features of the ship; it does of course have all the arrangements, usual in British construction, for a contamination-free citadel, shock protection and upper-deck washing down.

The main armament is the British Aerospace Sea Dart missile system. The Sea Dart is a third-generation surface-to-air missile which can engage either aircraft or missile targets. It is built round the Rolls-Royce Odin ramjet, and is 14ft (4.36m) long with a wingspan of 3ft (91cm) and a weight of 1,210lb (550kg). Guidance is by all-the-way semi-active homing, illumination of the target being provided by one of the two 909 radars in the ship. The missile works on the proportional-navigation principle, and, being supersonic and very agile, is suitable for engaging crossing as well as approaching targets. It is, therefore, an area defence weapon, able to defend ships other than the firing ship itself. Its range has not been released for publication. Launch and reloading rates are rapid, an important attribute when dealing with co-ordinated attacks attempting to swamp the defences. The Sea Dart can also be used against surface targets, probably out to horizon range.

To illustrate the complexity of such a system as well as the way in which British industry participates in its provision, a few sub-contractors may be mentioned: the guidance system is by Marconi Space and Defence Systems, the proximity fuze by EMI, control servos by Sperry. The list is not exhaustive.

The *Sheffield* Class also deploys the Lynx helicopter for anti-submarine, anti-surface ship and reconnaissance work; a single 4.5inch Mark 8 gun in a fully automatic mounting to provide a further channel of anti-aircraft fire as well as shore bombardment and surface action; and a shipborne torpedo weapon system for firing lightweight homing torpedoes against submarine targets detected by the ship's own sonar. Ship's sensors include Type 965R or Type 1022 air warning radar, Type 992Q target indication radar and Type 184 M sonar. These, with external information, feed into the ADAWS 5 computer system that is the heart of the modern and effective operations room.

With a ship's company of 280, the Sheffield Class have been called 'tight ships'. Analysis of comparable designs in other navies suggests that deck-space per man is less generous in the *Sheffield* than in most. Type 42 Ships' companies, in the main, reckon this is one of the hazards of the game. They are proud of the amount of firepower in their ships and would be unlikely to

swop it for more living space. No doubt, in any case, sailors from a generation back would be surprised by the comfort available in the accommodation of the *Sheffield* class.

Frigates

Before World War II ended, the attention of naval planners turned from the sturdy, mass-produced, relatively slow anti-submarine frigates that had provided so much convoy escort and support, to a ship capable of making the main anti-submarine contribution to the Fleet. Fleet speeds meant a slimmer hull and turbine propulsion, and the opportunity was taken to incorporate improved sonars and, later, a weapon-carrying helicopter. This was the genesis of the family of frigates that began with the *Whitby* (Type 12) and *Rothesay* classes, and culminated in the very successful *Leander* design. Though some ships of the *Rothesay* class are still serving, only the *Leanders* will be described in detail. After the *Leanders*, the line is continued in the *Broadsword* class (Type 22) although the family resemblances are harder to detect here. The *Amazon* class (Type 21) is a commercial design and of considerable interest for its deviations as well as its resemblances.

The *Leander Class*

In all, 26 ships of the Leander class were completed between 1963 and 1972. All were 372ft (113.4m) long; the first 16 had a beam of 41ft (12.5m) but the last 10 had two feet added to the beam for additional space and stability. In fact the *Leander* hull, with its fine entry and high freeboard, has proved exceptionally weatherly, and for their tonnage of 2,600 the class keep the sea particularly well.

The ships are powered by a proven system of two controlled superheat boilers and two sets of steam turbines giving 30,000 shaft horse power. Electrical power is provided by a standard combination of steam and diesel generators. The ships have twin rudders and are fitted with stabilisers. All these characteristics have been in the ships from the beginning, though the boilers were modified at a relatively early stage to burn diesel, rather than black, oil, thus simplifying logistic problems. The armament, however, has undergone major modifications during the mid-life refits of these ships. The programme began in 1972 and is expected to complete in 1984 or thereabouts.

The first batch of eight ships was modified principally by removing the 4.5inch twin gun turret and fitting in its place the Ikara anti-submarine missile system. The Ikara was developed jointly by the United Kingdom and Australia. It is, basically, a means of rapidly deploying a light anti-submarine torpedo in response to a sonar contact either from the ship's own medium-range sonar or from some unit in company. Missile trajectory is determined by a computer in the ship's operations room and passed to the missile in flight by a radio command link; the missile is monitored by a specialised control radar. At the computed

Right: The Leander hull shows its seakeeping qualities: HMS *Andromeda* in a seaway. *Crown Copyright*

Below: The first eight Leanders to be built were fitted with the Ikara anti-submarine missile during their mid-life modernisations. In this picture of HMS *Leander*, the Ikara can be seen in its circular mounting forward of the bridge. *Crown Copyright*

dropping point, the missile is commanded to release its torpedo, which parachutes into the water and starts an autonomous search for the submarine, homing and attacking when it gains contact.

The Ikara's range is given as 10 miles, which well matches the likely capabilities of the ship's own sonars in good conditions. The 184 M is a powerful active sonar giving a panoramic search in the surface duct, while the Variable Depth Sonar, towed astern of the ship, can be lowered to an optimum operating depth below the duct as determined by the ship's bathythermograph equipment. The Ikara has, of course, instant 24-hour availability to take advantage of these equipments' capabilities. The ship's Wasp helicopter can be regarded as a complementary anti-submarine weapon carrying system, as well of course as a performer of many other roles such as light transfers, visual surveillance and air-sea rescue. Finally, to complete the Ikara *Leanders'* comprehensive anti-submarine armament, they are still fitted with the Type 170 'searchlight' sonar and associated Limbo Mark 10 Mortar for attacking close-in submarine contacts.

For self-defence against air attack the Ikara *Leanders* have two quadruple Sea Cat launchers. These first-generation missiles made by Short Bros. have been fitted widely in HM Ships for many years, and their control systems have been extensively modified to improve their performance against aircraft and missiles. A separately-mounted director can be used to control one Sea Cat at a time; good Sea Cat aimers are prized possessions in any *Leander* ship's company. Rapid reloading can be done by hydraulic hoists. Sea Cat can also be used in the surface-to-surface role, as can the single 40mm Bofors guns mounted on either side of the bridge; once again, the ship's ability to carry out low-intensity operations cannot be neglected.

The second batch of narrow-beam *Leanders* have been fitted, instead of their 4.5inch guns, with four Exocet surface-to-surface missiles. They also have three quadruple Sea Cat launchers and the two 40mm Bofors remain. For anti-submarine work, provision has been made for a Lynx helicopter, which as the Wasp's successor provides more range, speed and endurance as

well as better weapons and avionics. This has meant removing the Limbo Mark 10 Mortar, but for close-range anti-submarine attack the ship has two sets of triple tubes – the ship-launched torpedo weapon system — armed with lightweight homing torpedoes, and the control equipment to go with them. Most ships of this batch no longer have the variable depth sonar.

Finally, most of the broad-beamed *Leanders* are in course of extensive modification. They will have Exocet in place of the 4.5in mounting, provision for a Lynx helicopter, and ship-launched torpedoes. But their air defence will be powerfully enhanced by the Sea Wolf system. This, described in detail below under the *Broadsword* Class, is the first true anti-missile missile. This version of the *Leanders* will, therefore, be able to approach ever more severe air defence environments in the 1980s and 1990s with a good deal of confidence, as well as keeping a powerful offensive punch both in the anti-submarine and anti-surface ship fields.

As the class characteristics have diverged, so to some extent have the sizes of *Leander* ships' companies. The Ikara ships have 240, the Exocet batch 230 and the modified broad-beamed type will have 260. All will live in air-conditioned accommodation which is well-planned and comfortable though by no means luxurious. Compared with ships of comparable size in some other navies, *Leander* ships' companies are large. This is a matter of deliberate policy and stems from the need, in the Admiralty Board's view, to be able to keep ships of the surface fleet manned for long periods in a state in which they can react instantly to threats of a varied and comprehensive kind. Clearly hands cannot all be kept at action stations that long, and consequently the ship's company must be large enough to man the vital weapon, control and machinery stations in the 'prime state' at defence watches.

Top left: HMS *Phoebe*, **one of the second batch of Leanders to be modernised, firing an Exocet missile.** *Crown Copyright*

Left: HMS *Sirius*, **an Exocet Leander, with her new Lynx helicopter ready to fly on.** *Crown Copyright*

Below: HMS *Andromeda*, **first of the broad-beam Leanders to be modernised, now has Sea Wolf and Exocet missile systems.** *Crown Copyright*

Aspects of life in a modern frigate

Top: HMS *Ariadne* floodlit on a visit to Sydney, Australia. *Crown Copyright*

Right: A view of the Panama Canal taken from HMS *Arethusa*; HMS *Juno* is in the background. *Crown Copyright*

Below right: On the bridge: the navigating officer – Lieutenant (now Commander) Haddacks – fixing the ship's position. *Crown Copyright*

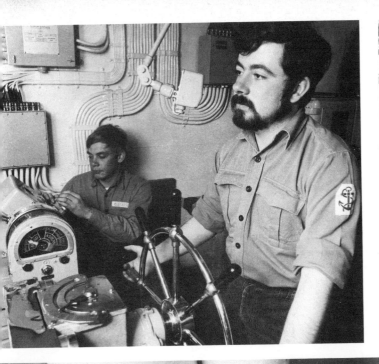

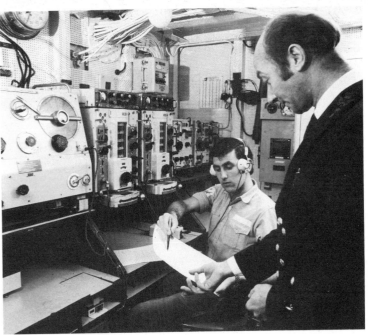

Above left: In the wheelhouse, the helmsman steers the ship. *Crown Copyright*

Above: In the communications centre: a signal is prepared for transmission. *Crown Copyright*

Left: In the engine room: MEA 1(P) O'Brien and Mech Preedy manning the throttles.
Crown Copyright

Above right: In the operations room: the Captain, surrounded by his plotting teams and advisers, during an exercise. All wear anti-flash clothing, as they would in action.
Crown Copyright

Right: In the junior ratings' dining hall, dinner and supper menus offer several choices. Facing the camera are ABs Eustice and Willingale and CEM Nolan. *Crown Copyright*

Below: On the upper deck: a light jackstay transfer with a Turkish destroyer during an exercise in the Mediterranean.
Official Photograph, Allied Naval Forces Southern Europe

The Broadsword Class

Originally conceived as a direct successor to the *Leander*, the *Broadsword* (Type 22) class developed into something a good deal more formidable and autonomous: as Antony Preston describes it, 'a big mid-ocean submarine-killer' of 3,560 tons. The reasons for this are complex, depending as they do on developments in weapon systems – both those fitted in the ship and those provided by other units – and the pattern of operations particularly in the anti-submarine field. The resultant is a ship whose chief characteristics are an ability to look after itself in a hot-war environment – operations at the higher level indeed — and offensive power particularly against submarines but also against surface units.

Taking the self-defence side of the ship first, this exists most notably in the Sea Wolf GWS 25 point defence system. This is a system full of innovation, and the most advanced so far in the world in meeting the threat from tactical missiles launched outside the range of the ship's own weapon systems. The requirements were clear enough when studies began in the late 1960s; quick reaction, a high kill probability, an ability to operate in all weathers and at night, and easy handling arrangements. The fundamental solution was to put all the complex equipment into the ship and keep the missile simple. This entailed telling it what to do throughout its trajectory. Government research establishments led on the project; British Aerospace, Marconi and Vickers were the chief contractors; the list of sub-contractors reads like a roll-call of the British electronics and armaments industry.

The operational sequence of a Sea Wolf firing starts with detection of the target by one of the special surveillance radars, Types 967/968. These are mounted back-to-back; 968 is a conventional E-band pulse radar for general surface and air warning, 967 a D-band radar whose pulse-doppler mode is specially suited to picking out fast-moving targets from a mass of stationary clutter. When these indicate a target to the Sea Wolf, one of the sextuple launchers slews rapidly to the bearing and as soon as the target is within effective range one or two missiles can be fired. These are quickly gathered into the beam of the 910 guidance radar, which is a monopulse system tracking both the target and the Sea Wolf missile(s) in a time multiplex mode. The 910 measures the angular difference between the Sea Wolf and the target and a command link issues course adjustments so that it closes the target accurately. The Sea Wolf explodes, by proximity or impact fuzing, as it flies by or actually hits the target.

Some interesting reported characteristics include great agility and supersonic speed in the Sea Wolf missile, the fact that it has hit a 4.5inch shell on trials, times from first detection to tracker alert as short as 2-3 seconds, and very handy, relatively light missiles (176lb-80kg) that can be treated as rounds of ammunition. Some less attractive features are heavy, hand-loaded launchers (though each carries six missiles in very weatherproof casings, and *Broadsword* has two, so is well off for ready-use ammunition), the need for a supplementary television tracker for very low-level targets, and the need for no less than five computers to form the guidance shaping unit. These may be the inevitable price of excellence, or they may be first-generation features that can be improved. Certainly the system is one of great potential and gives promise of secure self-defence for surface ships.

Apart from the 967/968 radars, the *Broadsword* class are provided with highly adequate sensors in other modes: electronic warfare equipment including an ability to conduct signal analysis and direction-finding in the 1-18 GHz range; navigational radar; the sensors carried by the Lynx helicopter; and the new Type 2016 sonar, a medium-range set which by advanced analysis

Below: The principles of Sea Wolf guidance. Angular differences between the missile and target are measured, and the missile ordered to alter course accordingly through a command radio link. *Marconi/Vickers/British Aerospace Dynamics Group*

Bottom: HMS *Broadsword*, first of the Type 22 frigates. She has four Exocet missiles forward. The forward Sea Wolf mounting is prominent, in white, immediately abaft these. Sea Wolf control radars can be seen forward of the foremast and abaft the mainmast. *Crown Copyright*

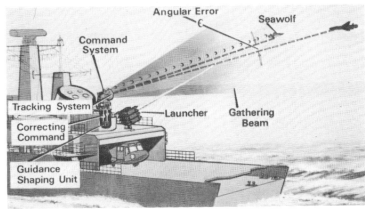

techniques provides a much better answer than hitherto to the age-old anti-submarine operator's question, 'Is that a submarine or not?' All these feed into a centralised operations room that seems to have struck the balance, long sought, between trying to tell the command what it should do – and thus stifling initiative – and supplying it with out-of-date and insufficient information – this giving it no scope to use its initiative anyway. This new system – fitted, by the way, into other new and modernised construction as well as the Type 22 – is called the Computer Aided Action Information System (CAAIS) which precisely describes its purpose of doing the donkey work of computation, collation, cross-feeding, comparison and display while leaving decisions where they belong. It is a modular system employing the most modern microprocessing techniques. Ferranti are the prime contractors.

The *Broadsword* class can, therefore, exercise command functions at sea, and this may turn out to be an important part of its role. But it can also take the offensive in many situations. It has four Exocet surface-to-surface missiles, ship-mounted torpedo tubes for anti-submarine action and stowage for two Lynx helicopters which can fulfil a variety of tasks in surface and anti-submarine work. In peacetime, it is likely that only one Lynx will be carried. Finally, the gun is not totally neglected: there are two 40mm Bofors.

Many of the basic characteristics of this class are shared with the *Sheffield* class destroyers. Power plants are identical and auxiliary machinery very similar. Robustness, in the shape of good redundancy of equipment, anti-contamination arrangements and well-protected magazines, is similar too. Size is a little larger than the *Sheffield's*, and the apparently inevitable lengthening of later hulls is planned for the *Broadswords* from hull No5 onwards. Because of their bigger size and rather smaller ship's complement – 224 against 280 – the *Broadsword* class are roomier than the *Sheffield*, and indeed are probably as spacious as any frigates in the world. Such space has a way of being filled up with fighting and ancillary equipment as the years pass, and the *Broadswords* have to last a long time.

Below: HMS *Alacrity*, of the Amazon Class, is bidden farewell by the band of the 3rd Battalion the Royal Green Jackets after a visit to the British Sovereign Base Area in Cyprus. HMS *Galatea* and a RAF helicopter are in the background. The workboat and Mexeflote belong to No 10 Port Squadron, RCT. *RAF photograph: Crown Copyright*

Right: The 4.5in (113mm) Mark 8 Gun system fitted in the Sheffield and Amazon classes. *Vickers Armament Division*

Muzzle Brake
Reduces recoil force, producing a shorter recoil which saves space and allows a significant weight reduction.

Fume Extractor
Clears the barrel between rounds eliminating necessit for air blast system.

The Amazon *Class*
While planning for the Type 22 was still going through its unexpectedly slow evolution, a need arose to keep up frigate numbers by new construction, and consequently a private-venture design by Vosper Thorneycroft and Yarrow was put into effect. This turned out to be a general-purpose frigate with the racy, yacht-like lines that have been associated for many years with the Southampton firm. The *Amazon* class (Type 21), as they are called, were completed between 1974 and 1978.

They are 384ft (117m) long, 41.7ft (12.7m) beam and displace 2,815 tons. The machinery is the now familiar Olympus-Tyne fit driving controllable-pitch propellers; in fact *Amazon* was the first ship into service in the Royal Navy with this type of propulsion. Sensors include radars Type 992 Q for general warning, 978 for navigation and GWS 24 for Sea Cat control; sonar Type 184 M; and an electronic warfare fit. Weapon systems consist of four Exocet (from hull No4 onwards), the Lynx helicopter, two 20mm Oerlikon guns, and three systems which need more detailed treatment under this heading: the 4.5inch Mark 8 single gun, the Ship Launched Torpedo Weapon System (in certain ships only) and the Corvus Broadband Chaff Rocket.

The Vickers 4.5inch Mark 8 gun, also fitted in the *Sheffield* class, is provided for surface action, for naval gunfire support of land forces, and to provide a channel of anti-aircraft fire. The main feature which distinguishes it from previous 4.5inch

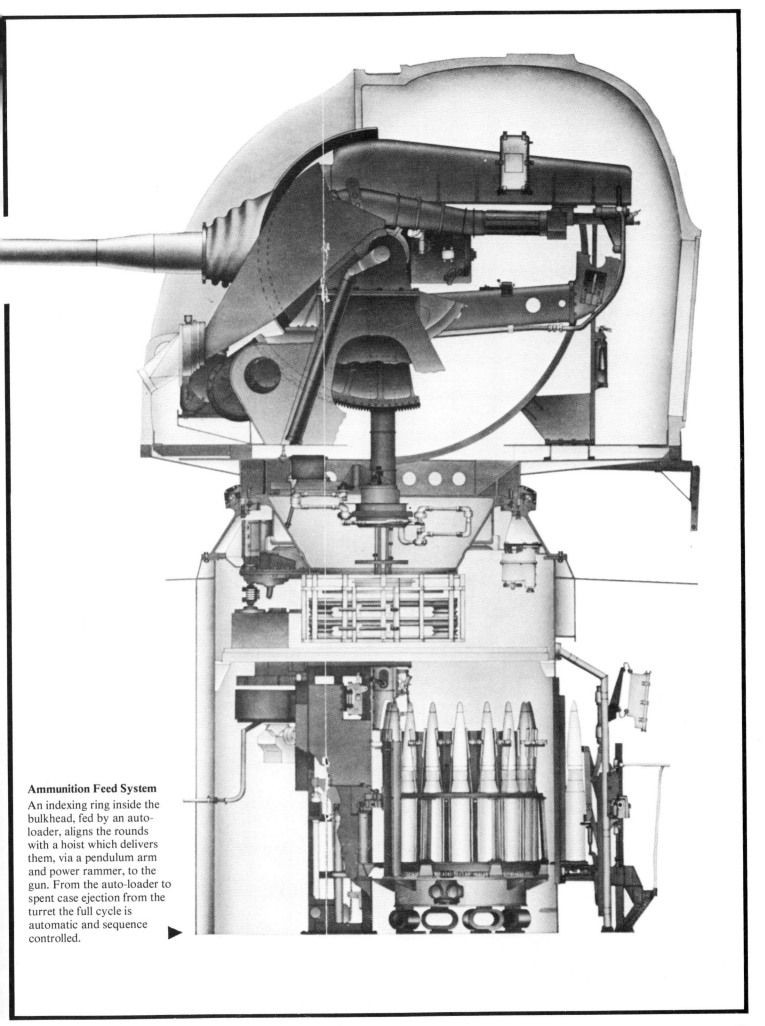

Ammunition Feed System
An indexing ring inside the bulkhead, fed by an auto-loader, aligns the rounds with a hoist which delivers them, via a pendulum arm and power rammer, to the gun. From the auto-loader to spent case ejection from the turret the full cycle is automatic and sequence controlled.

▶

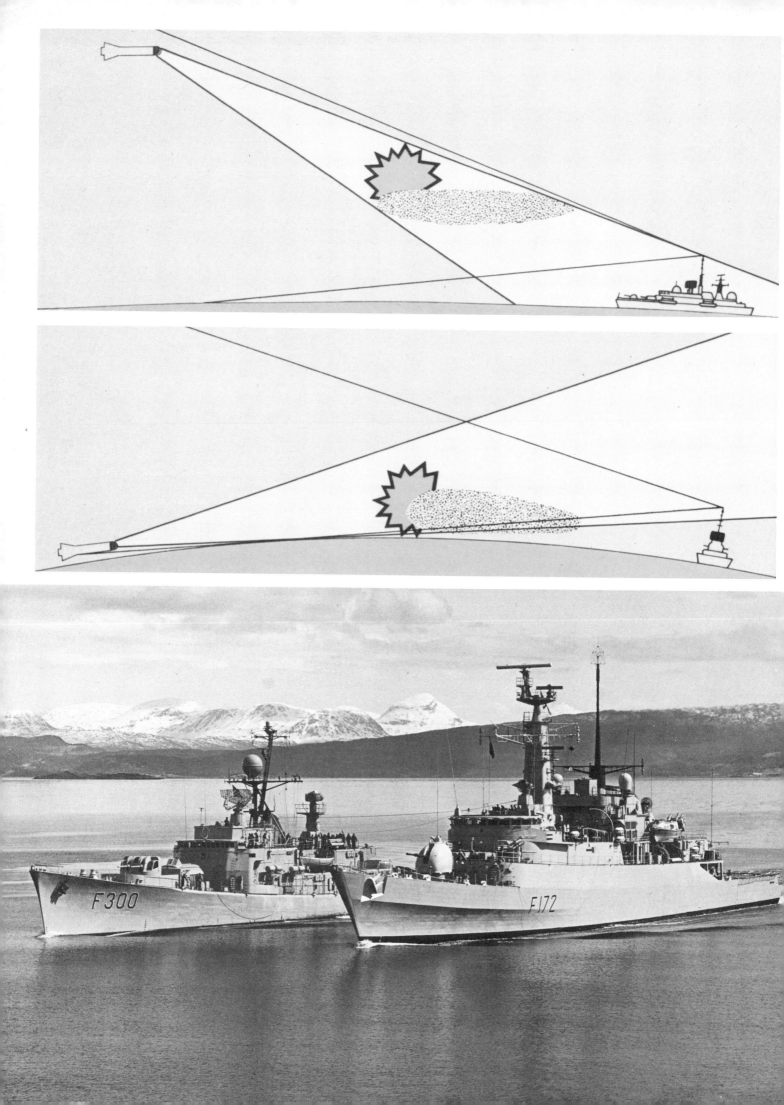

Above left: **Corvus Broadband Chaff Rocket: possible modes of operation against diving or sea-skimming missiles. The ship releases a cloud of 'window' chaff which causes the missile to explode harmlessly.**
Plessey Aerospace/Vickers Shipbuilding Group Limited

Left: **Type 21 frigates have played a full part in NATO exercises and deployments. HMS *Ambuscade* and HNMS *Oslo* off Norway when both were operating with the NATO Standing Naval Force, Atlantic (STANAVFORLANT).** *Crown Copyright*

Above: **In the ship control centre, HMS *Amazon*. Automatic monitoring of all the electrical and mechanical services of the ship allows manpower to be kept to a minimum.** *Crown Copyright*

systems is a fully automatic turret which can, when the gun is preloaded, carry out an engagement with no one in the turret. Reaction times, whether the turret is manned or not, are very short, and the accuracies claimed in all modes are high. Flexibility of ammunition supply ensures that roles can be changed rapidly. The gun itself, developed by the Armament Research and Development Establishment, is designed for long barrel life.

The Ship Launched Torpedo Weapon System (its unlovely acronym is STWS-1) is standard also in *Sheffield*, *Broadsword* and some modified *Leander* classes. It consists of three torpedo tubes mounted on either side of the ship, each capable of launching by compressed air a lightweight homing torpedo of the Mark 46 or, later, the Stingray type. Equipment in the operations room gives the torpedo initial course, depth and search instructions. Since the torpedoes themselves are primarily airborne weapons they will be described in Chapter V.

The Corvus Broadband Chaff Rocket, manufactured by Plessey Aerospace, is a purely self-defence system, but in an age of homing missiles may turn out to be an important one. It is standard equipment in British naval new construction. Its aim is to divert incoming missiles by generating areas remote from the ship that will give radar responses more attractive to home on. Rockets are fired which dispense metallised chaff strips, cut to match the operating frequency of the missile's radar seeker, in a cloud that either masks the firing ship or appears in a place at some distance from it. Firing may be carried out before an incoming missile is detected, on electronic indications that it is about to be launched; or it may be left until the attack develops; or both modes may be used. The whole system is made much more effective by the computer assistance that a modern operations room provides. Strong nerves and quick thinking help, too.

In the design of the Type 21 special effort was made to cut manpower to the minimum consistent with prolonged prime state manning. Automated weapon systems and specially designed action information equipment, centralised stores arrangements and machinery control, were all part of this drive, and it resulted in a complement of 170, a considerable saving. This has had two results. The ships are particularly comfortable to live in; and there is a very strong small-ship loyalty in the *Amazon* class. The design has come under some criticism in the Press for its light scantlings, including aluminium upperworks, and lack of margin for either action damage or mid-life modernisation. But those who have served in these ships regard them as well-balanced and effective units, and defend them stoutly. It is probably right to say that they are particularly good for peacetime and not-quite-war conditions; in the jargon, they are optimised to low-intensity operations. They have certainly played a full part in Fleet activities since coming into service.

Assault Ships

The strangest-looking surface ships in the Fleet are the Assault Ships *Fearless* and *Intrepid*, which double their amphibious roles with that of giving sea training to midshipmen from the Britannia Royal Naval College, Dartmouth. They displace 12,000 tons, are 520ft (158m) long and have a beam of 80ft (24.4m). Their main feature is a dock area aft, leading to a tank deck forward within the ship. The dock can be flooded by controlled ballasting, and vehicles of all kinds driven into landing craft waiting in the dock; when loaded, they can float out through the stern. The ships carry eight landing craft, four at davits and four in the dock.

On the upper deck level there is a large flight deck aft which can operate two helicopters at a time, and park more if operations are not taking place. There is, however, no helicopter hangar. Conventional armament is confined to four Sea Cat launchers and two 40mm Bofors guns. The operations room and communications complex are custom-made for commanding an amphibious landing.

The ship's normal complement is 580, including about 90 Royal Marines, but this varies with the current role. An infantry battalion or Royal Marines Commando can be embarked, together with their equipment; but it might equally be a tank squadron or unit of the Royal Engineers. In the training role, up to 150 midshipmen can be embarked.

These unusual ships are a good example of the way surface units can be adapted and made more versatile. Originally intended to support 'brush-fire wars' east of Suez, they are now valued components of the NATO forces in the Eastern Atlantic area and valuable platforms for training tomorrow's officers.

Right: HMS *Fearless*, **built for the carriage of mechanised units in amphibious warfare but capable of a variety of roles including Midshipmen's training.** *Crown Copyright*

Below: All ships of the surface fleet have washdown equipment to clear the upper deck surfaces of contamination after nuclear, chemical or biological attack. HMS *Intrepid* **during an exercise off Portland.** *Crown Copyright*

Some recent retirements

Above left: HMS *Bulwark*, a former fixed-wing carrier, was converted to the commando role in 1960. She was placed in reserve in 1976 but reactivated in early 1979, and served with the Fleet until mid-1981. *Crown Copyright*

Left: Finally withdrawn from service in 1979, HMS *Ark Royal* represented during the previous quarter-century a comprehensive above-water fighting capability. *Crown Copyright*

Above: The last 6-in guns in the Royal Navy firing on board the helicopter cruiser HMS *Blake*. Originally a conventional gun cruiser, *Blake* was extensively modified aft to carry four Sea King helicopters. She retired in 1979. *Crown Copyright*

Above right: The County class destroyer HMS *London*, which will not be modernised, alongside HMS *Belfast*, on exhibition in the Pool of London. *Crown Copyright*

Right: HMS *Gurkha*, a frigate of the Tribal class which left service in the late 1970s. *Crown Copyright*

Below right: HMS *Londonderry*, given a new mast layout and distinctive profile as a communication and radar trials ship. Her type 12 hull is unchanged. She will also be used for navigation training. *Crown Copyright*

The Future

As the text of this book reaches its deadline, a White Paper on *The United Kingdom Defence Programme: The Way Forward* has just been published. It was not, of course, unheralded; the media had been full of speculation for months. The changes now projected for the surface Fleet in the next decade are not, therefore, a total surprise nor (after all the rumour) a totally unpleasant one. Before outlining them, it is worth mentioning some of the salient factors that must have been matters of debate, as well as some common ground.

First, there is pretty general agreement that surface ships have an important role in normal peacetime conditions, in what we have called low-intensity operations and in higher-level operations of limited scale. The more the United Kingdom regards its interests, both in the NATO area and outside it, as protected by such operations, the more emphasis it will necessarily put on surface ships. In so far as a proportion of the surface Fleet can be optimised to such operations, it will need less of the complicated and expensive weaponry that enables it to fight at the highest level.

The main debate, then, must have been about higher-level operations in the NATO area and the part of surface ships in them. It is NATO's aim to use the sea for the passage of trans-Atlantic and cross-Channel reinforcements, for the deployment of amphibious forces where necesssary, and for the continued stationing of the ultimate deterrent in ballistic missile submarines. The threat to those uses comes from Soviet submarines, many of them nuclear-powered and missile-armed; from Soviet aircraft, both reconnaissance and strike; and from Soviet surface units, which are increasing all the time in number and potency.

There is a view that all these threats can be contained by submarines and aircraft, the latter in air defence, strike/attack and anti-submarine modes. It can be argued that not only is technology on their side – giving them good weapon systems, the ability to make a quick getaway, and sufficient communications and co-ordination – but also geography; the Greenland-Iceland-UK gap, if not fully sealable, is at least a good choke point if well guarded.

Against this view it can be contended that historically, reliance on such distant protection operations has generally proved disastrous; it has been necessary to fight all round the areas of sea to be used. In such operations the relative effectiveness of surface ships, and of their embarked aircraft, increases and that of submarines and shore-based aircraft decreases. Moreover, pre-deployment of Soviet forces could pre-empt any attempt to seal the gaps. Thus, proponents of the surface ship argue, there is still a requirement for powerful surface forces to provide the defence-in-depth needed for sea use.

There is, however, another dimension to the debate. This, of great importance when budgets are tight, is that of quality – particularly of destroyer and frigate type ships. The more sophisticated of these are now very expensive; a figure of £120million a copy is quoted for the Type 22. And however good their systems, and however staunch they may be for their size, a good many of them will not survive their first battle, if it comes to that.(Neither will similar Soviet surface forces do better). The question then is whether a proportion at least of these medium-sized surface ships should not be of a simpler kind, cheaper in capital cost, manpower and running expenses, so that numbers could be kept up. Capabilities for peacetime and low-intensity operations would not be affected; they might even be enhanced, by the provision of less weighty, and therefore more usable, weapon systems.

The resolution of the debate by the present Government is best described by the following quotation from the White Paper: '. . . for the future the most cost-effective maritime mix – the best-balanced operational contribution for our situation – will be one which continues to enhance our maritime-air and submarine effort, but accepts a reduction below current plans in the size of our surface fleet and the scale and sophistication of new ship-building, and breaks away from the practice of costly mid-life modernisation.'

In consequence, plans put forward in the White Paper seek to sustain a figure of about 50 destroyers and frigates (eight of them in the Stand-By Squadron) as against the 59 now declared to NATO. The entry into service of simpler, cheaper frigates to a new design (the Type 23) will be accelerated. Furthermore, although all three carriers will be completed, only two will be kept in service at any one time. Specialist amphibious shipping will be phased out rather earlier than was originally planned.

This leaner surface Fleet seems likely, however, to spend a higher proportion of its time in the more exotic parts of the world. Substantial task group deployments for exercises and visits in the South Atlantic, Caribbean, Indian Ocean or further east are likely to take place regularly.

Two technical innovations, one in the medium and one in the much longer term, could change the face of the surface Fleet considerably. The first is the surface-ship passive sonar towed array: a device that may greatly increase the anti-submarine reach of surface units. The tactics of units other than towed-array ships, including anti-submarine helicopters, may be profoundly altered. The second, even more revolutionary, is the possibility of a ship-mounted high-energy laser for self-defence against missiles. The scientific problems of attenuation and thermal blooming, and the technical problem of pointing the beam accurately enough to damage an incoming missile, are immense but not insoluble; the necessary vast outlay of resources for research is possible only to the USA (and USSR) but it is not out of the question that if a breakthrough is made in the US, the technology will be made available to Britain. The advantage of such a system, of course, would lie in the virtual inexhaustability of the 'magazine', which would be the ship's electrical generating system.

In summary, the present surface Fleet has aimed at high quality and sufficient numbers. Both numbers and quality will drop off somewhat in the next decade on the newly presented plans, but even in 1990 it will still be a capable force that can give pause to a potential aggressor. Imagination and ingenuity will be needed to seize upon any new development that gives the prospect of enhanced fighting power for little cost. Whatever happens in the weapon field, co-ordination of all the means for offensive action, for force and group defence and for electronic warfare will remain operationally crucial. Only in this way can the potential for defence in depth, on both sides of the sea-air interface, be realised. The command and information systems of British ships, and the training of their companies, must remain capable of that task.

5

The Fleet Air Arm

No part of the Naval service has been so swept by changes in policy, control and resource allocation as the Fleet Air Arm. Differences between genuinely-held and logically-expressed views on how maritime air power should be based, deployed and operated have existed since aircraft first flew over the sea, and have been argued with warmth, indeed passion; they have resulted, when compounded with political factors, in several radical changes of command, organisation and structure since 1918.

It is not the writer's intention to rake over any coals. But some brief account of Governmental decisions since the mid-1960s is necessary to explain the present structure of the Fleet Air Arm.

In 1964 the incoming Government initiated a Review of Britain's defences and in early 1966 announced its decision on one of the crucial issues raised in that Review: the future of carriers operating high-performance fixed-wing aircraft. The Royal Navy at the time had four such ships, all ageing; the first of a new class was ordered. The Review said that the only task specific to such a ship was the landing or withdrawal of troops against opposition outside the range of land-based strike aircraft; no such operations were envisaged without allies, and the requirement was

accordingly to lapse. £1,000 million, at the prices of those days, would be saved.

The other tasks attributable to the aircraft of the fixed-wing carrier needed, though, to be re-allocated. They had, after all, sought to control the airspace and sea's surface out to some hundreds of miles, and the inner space beneath the sea out to some tens of miles, from the carrier and ships in company with it. If sea power was to mean anything, in the NATO context as much as any other, the job still needed doing and aircraft were still needed to do much of it.

The solution arrived at, after considerable discussion and adjustment during the next half-decade, was that in the deep field, some hundreds of miles from a group of ships requiring air cover, the responsibility of air defence and anti-surface ship strike would rest with Royal Air Force high-performance aircraft

Below: '. . . The V/STOL fixed wing aircraft . . . emerged as a requirement . . .' A Sea Harrier takes off from HMS *Invincible*'s ski jump. Photo by HMS *Invincible*. *Crown Copyright*

operating from bases in the United Kingdom, and as before anti-submarine air cover in that area would be provided by long range maritime patrol aircraft of the RAF. Closer in, the brunt of anti-submarine air operations would be taken by shipborne helicopters, both light weapon- and sensor-carriers and heavy hunter-killers; and anti-surface ship and air defence (which at this point would tend to mean anti-missile defence) would depend on shipborne resources. There was, clearly, considerable scope for overlap between the deep and close fields, but this was fully in accord with the ideas of inter-service co-operation and of defence in depth. There was, equally clearly, a need for a platform to deploy the larger anti-submarine helicopters and to exert on-the-spot control of operations, and as we have seen this evolved into the *Invincible* class.

There was still a difficulty in the above-water area. Royal Air Force resources, charged also with the air defence of the United Kingdom, were likely to find themselves hard pressed; they might not be able to react in sufficient time or strength to attacks on the Fleet by regiments of fast, missile-armed aircraft even in the Eastern Atlantic area. Moreover, the Fleet might find it necessary to operate beyond the range of RAF strike and air defence aircraft. There was, therefore, a need for shipborne air resources to detect and disrupt so far as possible the approach and organisation of enemy air or surface forces in these circumstances. The V/STOL fixed-wing aircraft, with its ability to shoot down shadowers, probe and strike at surface ships, and intercept suspicious air contacts, emerged as a requirement to fill this need.

There were, of course, requirements for embarked aircraft in circumstances far removed from the classic, Eastern Atlantic case. Most of them could be filled by helicopers and V/STOL aircraft in other roles; for example, anti-submarine helicopters can help in disaster relief, and V/STOL aircraft can carry out shore reconnaissance or ground attack in limited coastal operations. But for landing troops in numbers, as the specialist reinforcement forces of the United Kingdom still require, troop-carrying helicopters are needed.

The Royal Navy's aircraft therefore split into four main categories. There are two kinds of anti-submarine helicopters: light for weapon-carrying and general duties, with some ability to carry sensors, embarked in destroyers and frigates; and heavy for detecting, localising and killing submarines, embarked in carriers and, latterly, Fleet Auxiliaries. There are troop-carrying helicopters embarked in ships in the commando role. And finally there are V/STOL fixed-wing aircraft to carry out air defence probe and attack duties from the carriers.

Anti-submarine Helicopters

The potential of the helicopter as a shipborne vehicle was recognised early in the Royal Navy and a helicopter in fact flew from SS *Daghestan* in 1944 on an Atlantic convoy. There was no doubt, in the minds of the joint UK/US board that commissioned the trial, that the future of the seaborne helicopter would be intimately bound up with anti-submarine work, and its value would lie essentially in improving the anti-submarine reach of the ship that carried it. At that time the technology of weapons, sensors and helicopters themselves did not exist to realise that potential; but it progressed remarkably quickly, particularly in the hands of the Americans, so that by the early 1950s helicopters were being flown from ships to deploy sonars which they 'dunked' in the water, and to carry weapons to distant submarine contacts.

Below: HMS *Aurora*'**s Wasp helicopter returns on board.** *Official photograph, Allied Naval Forces Southern Europe*

Below right: A Wasp takes off into the sunset. *Crown Copyright*

Small Ships' Helicopters

The Royal Navy had approached the possibility of flying helicopters from destroyers and frigates, particularly those in the 2-3,000ton range, with some caution. However, by the late 1950s a prototype helicopter, the P 531, light and small enough for small-ship decks and hangars was flying, as a private venture by Saunders-Roe (later Westland Aircraft). With help from the Royal Aircraft Establishment, particularly on deck-landing and securing arrangements, this developed into the Wasp HAS Mark 1, and ships of the *Leander* class carried such aircraft from 1964 onwards. They subsequently embarked in the *Tribal*, *Rothesay* (on modification) and *Hecla* classes, and HMS *Endurance*.

The Wasp is distinguished externally by its long-legged, four-footed undercarriage, large cabin, and unbuttoned-looking engine. With a main rotor diameter of only 32ft 3in (9.78m) and a length of 30ft 4in (9.2m) it is handy for deck operation, particularly with the simple swivel-link 'hold-on-deck' and release gear provided to secure it. Its single Rolls-Royce Nimbus engine gives 685 shaft horse power. As with all aircraft, range and payload are interchangeable to some extent, but the Wasp with a pilot and aircrewman up has a typical range of over 180 miles, or an endurance of two hours or so.

It can carry two anti-submarine torpedoes, and this of course is its chief operational task: given an anti-submarine contact, either from its own ship's or someone else's sensors, it can fly to the target area and drop one or both weapons to conduct their autonomous search and attack. For most of its life the Wasp carried Mark 44 torpedoes but can now carry the US Mark 46. This is a 12.75inch (324mm) diameter torpedo weighing 513lb (233kg) propelled by a five-cylinder liquid-fuelled motor and having an active-passive acoustic homing head. Its acquisition range is reckoned by the technical journals to be about 500yards (460m). While the torpedo's search patterns increase its radius of effectiveness once in the water, it can be seen that considerable accuracy in directing and flying the Wasp is necessary for a successful attack.

The Wasp can alternatively be armed with depth charges for anti-submarine work or with two Nord AS-12 missiles for attacking surface craft. These are wire-guided, visually-sighted missiles weighing 165lb (75kg) with a range of up to 6,500 yards (6,000m). For rescue work, the Wasp is fitted with a winch and some notable Wasp rescues have been carried out in the open sea. It can also, of course, carry out personnel and light cargo transfers. Finally, it is a visual reconnaissance vehicle which can go out (and up) and look beyond the ship's own horizon.

For a first-generation small-ship helicopter the Wasp in fact did nobly, and its parent squadron, 829 at Portland, could be proud of the consistently high performance of ships' flights. But the next generation was to offer many improvements and advantages.

This development, led initially by Westland Aircraft Limited but joined by Sud-Aviation in France, was originally called the WG 13 and subsequently the Lynx. It began in the mid-1960s – such are the lead-times in modern aircraft systems – and the prototype flew in 1971. The Intensive Flying Trials Unit, with participation by the Royal Netherlands Navy since they were buying a version of the aircraft, formed in September 1976 and the first ship's flight embarked in December 1977. Deliveries have proceeded at a steady pace and by October 1980, 23 Lynx flights were nominated to ships.

The Lynx HAS Mark 2 is of slightly hump-backed appearance with a prominent snub nose and a tricycle fixed undercarriage. It has a four-bladed semi-rigid rotor (which of course folds for stowage) with a diameter of 42 feet (12.74m); its length, with rotors turning, is 49ft 9in (15.90m). With these dimensions, and a weight nearly double that of the Wasp, it requires rather more spacious flight deck arrangements than its predecessor, and a more sophisticated deck securing mechanism. This is provided by the Harpoon, a hydraulically operated retractable prong in the

Left: The Lynx, new generation small-ship helicopter, seen here with a prototype in company. *Crown Copyright*

Below left: The Lynx Intensive Flying Trials Unit at RNAS Yeovilton was a joint venture by the Royal Navy and Royal Netherlands Navy. The two middle helicopters here are RNLN aircraft. Photo by Leading Airman (Phot) L. A. McKenzie, HMS *Heron*. *Crown Copyright*

Right: The first deck landing of a production Lynx helicopter on HMS *Birmingham* in 1977. Photo by Leading Airman Nigel Thomas. *Crown Copyright*

Below: The Sea Skua air-to-surface missile carried by the Lynx: operational sequence. *British Aerospace Dynamic Group*

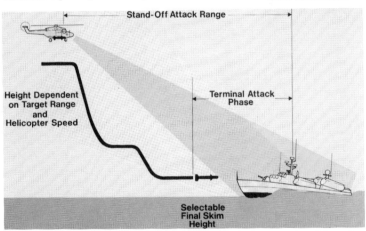

underside of the Lynx which engages in a honeycomb grid on the flight deck. This can hold the helicopter against a 35° roll.

Power is provided by two Rolls-Royce Gem engines of 830 shaft horse power take-off rating, driving through three interconnecting gearboxes to the rotors and auxiliary services. This is a fast helicopter, with a maximum cruise speed of 150 knots (270km/hr), and for a light helicopter its endurance is good: a typical operating profile gives a time on task 50 nautical miles from the ship, with a full anti-submarine weapon load, of 1 hour 55 minutes.

If it is proper to speak of the Lynx as having a primary role, this is still anti-submarine weapon-carrying; the Lynx can deliver two torpedoes of the Mark 46 or, later, the Stingray type, or depth charges. To help it in this task it has, as well as parent ship direction, an impressive array of avionics: an autopilot, VHF/UHF radio, the Decca Tactical Air Navigation System (TANS) with doppler inputs, a frequency-agile search radar, IFF (Interrogation Friend or Foe), and an I-band transponder.

But anti-submarine weapon-carrying is only one role of this versatile helicopter. It can carry up to nine passengers as well as

the pilot and observer; or up to 2,000lb (909kg) of internal freight; or, for casualty evacuation, three stretcher cases and a medical attendant. It can, of course, carry out air-sea rescue; indeed the first six Lynx for the Royal Netherlands Navy were supplied primarily for that role.

Finally, however, the Lynx introduces a new dimension into small ship helicopter operations by its combination of the Sea Spray radar and Sea Skua missile for attacking surface craft. The Sea Spray is a lightweight (145lb-66kg) I-band, frequency-agile radar optimised to detect and track small surface craft. Its presentation to the observer is made by a specially bright TV raster display which can also show information in numerical form. When it is used to track a target for the Sea Skua missile, the Sea Spray uses a monopulse mode the details of which have not been released. The Sea Skua is a semi-active homing missile which homes on echoes from a target illuminated by the Sea Spray radar. On release from the helicopter it drops under autopilot control to a preselected sea-skimming height, and on acquiring the target homes by proportional navigation, delivering a 44lb (20kg) warhead. The missile's range has not been released, but can be expected to be substantially better than that of the AS-12, thus displacing the helicopter further from enemy missiles and anti-aircraft fire. Combined with the advantages of a sea-skimming trajectory and all-weather operation, this is a significant advance in the over-the-horizon power of surface units. The small size of the warhead is not such a disadvantage as might appear since, first, each Lynx can carry four Sea Skuas and fire them in rapid succession; and, second, damage to upper-deck gear, not least radars, is an important way of incapacitating a modern ship, or greatly reducing its effectiveness. The Sea Skua is remarkably compact, being only 8ft 2in (2.5m) long and weighing some 165lb (75kg).

The success of the Lynx as a multirole helicopter is indicated by the fact that over 300 are on order, or delivered, in 10 countries; and its potential is shown by the fact that already in some countries' versions it carries dunking sonar, sonobuoys and uprated engines.

Large Anti-submarine Helicopters

Deployment of large anti-submarine helicopters in the Royal Navy dates from the middle 1950s. The helicopters, which at that time could carry a sensor or a weapon but not both, were basically American designs from the Sikorsky company but manufactured under licence by Westland Aircraft. This pattern has continued, although the divergences between succeeding British and American designs have tended to widen.

The Royal Navy is now into its third generation of such helicopters. The first, the Whirlwind, requires no mention in this book since it is no longer operated by the RN. The second, the Wessex, is still extant in the ships' flights of the County class destroyers in the HAS Mark 3 version. But since its dimensions are similar to those of the Mark 5 troop-carrying version, of which more detail follows, they need no mention here. The Wessex 3 carries a dunking sonar and can in addition carry two homing torpedoes, and it has good aids for both navigation and aircraft control in the hover, but on the airframe and with the limited single engine power available, endurance is short when compared with its much more effective successor.

This is the Sea King HAS Mark 2, which began to come into service in 1975 and absorbed Sea Kings HAS Mark 1, in service since 1970, as they were modified to Mark 2 standard. It is, roughly, a ten-tonner; maximum take-off weight is 21,000lb (9545kg). Rotor diameter is 62ft (18.8m) and length with rotors turning 57ft 2in (17.3m). The power plant consists of two 1,660 shaft horse power Rolls-Royce Gnome H 1400-1 turboshaft engines. Power supplies are comprehensive, as they need to be for the avionics: doppler navigation, search radar, radio altimeter, compass, homing equipment, and two devices which need rather more description, the dunking sonar and the automatic flight control system.

The dunking sonar, suspended by a cable from the Sea King and capable of being hauled up into it, is a Plessey Type 195 set whose main mode is active. It gives 360° coverage in four 90° steps; bearing accuracy is achieved by the use of multiple beams in each 90° sector. Extensive use is made of the doppler effect – which causes a frequency shift in the echo from a moving target – for classification, that is sorting out submarine from non-submarine echoes. The operator can control the depth of the transducer, thus being able to select the optimum depth for the water conditions of the day. A ship can do this with a variable depth sonar, but she is then tactically restricted by having to tow it about. A helicopter is either hovering with its sonar in the water, or in transit to a new dunking position with its sonar raised.

Below: A Sea King anti-submarine helicopter from HMS *Hermes* **preparing to dip its sonar.** *Crown Copyright*

Two frigates of the Royal Navy task group on patrol in the Gulf of Oman, HMS *Alacrity* **(F174) and HMS** *Naiad* **(F39) flanking the fleet tanker RFA** *Blue Rover* **(A270).**
Crown Copyright, HQ C-in-C Fleet

Left: Royal Marine ski troops being drawn along by a BV 202 Bandwagon oversnow vehicle. The helicopter is a Wessex 5. *Crown Copyright*

Top: The nuclear-powered fleet submarine HMS *Churchill* in Scottish waters. *Vickers Shipbuilding Group*

Above: HMS *Battleaxe*, second of the Type 22 frigate class. She is armed with Exocet surface-to-surface and Sea Wolf surface-to-air missiles and can carry two Lynx helicopters. *Crown Copyright*

A Sea Harrier FRS 1 of No 801 Naval Air
Squadron aboard HMS *Invincible* in June 1981.
Denis J. Calvert

Above: The Sea King can carry weapons and sonobuoys as well as sonar and so is a self-contained anti-submarine search and attack system. Photo by Leading Airman (Phot) Colin Whatmore.
Crown Copyright

Left: The Observer of a Sea King helicopter, a key member of the search and attack team who acts as its tactical director and is often the captain of the aircraft. *Crown Copyright*

Below left: Stingray torpedoes under construction. *Marconi Space and Defence Systems, Limited*

The efficient conduct of these two simple-sounding operations is the business of the automatic flight control system. This was developed and is still built by Louis Newmark. When the helicopter goes into the hover, height and horizontal movement are fed into a computer by a radar altimeter and doppler radar respectively. The computer, working through servos, works the controls so that the helicopter comes to the correct height for dunking and is stationary over the sea. Once the sonar is lowered another set of sensing devices, surrounding the sonar cable, feeds into the computer so that the cable is kept vertical.

All these aids are of great importance when operating a relatively long-endurance helicopter like the Sea King, which can stay on task for over four hours on a routine anti-submarine screening mission. The crew – two pilots, an observer and an aircrewman – can save their energies for the times when it matters, when they classify a contact as a submarine and go in to attack. For the Sea King can carry out both search and attack roles; it carries either four depth charges or, more usually, four Mark 44 or 46 torpedoes. The latter will shortly be superseded by the British-made Stingray torpedo.

The Stingray, produced by Marconi Space and Defence Systems, has very similar dimensions to the Mark 46 but has a much more sophisticated homing head. This is said to incorporate a multimode, multibeam sonar feeding into a computer of great capacity and flexibility. The software which can be put into the computer, and kept up to date as intelligence and experience allow, should ensure that classification of the target is extremely reliable and that false targets – whether fortuitous or deliberately released by the submarine – are rejected. Excellent deep and shallow water performance is claimed, and the computer will even tell its torpedo what sonar modes and attack tactics to adopt once the target is located and classified. Much research and development money has been invested in the Stingray and it should prove, as it is claimed to be, the best lightweight anti-submarine torpedo in the world. It will be fitted not only to all anti-submarine helicopters but to RAF Nimrod long range maritime patrol aircraft and in surface ships for firing by the STWS system.

Finally, some Sea King helicopters are fitted with a passive 'Jezebel' sonobuoy system, and in due course the whole Sea King fleet will be equipped with the Lightweight Acoustic Processing and Display System (LAPADS) and called Sea King HAS Mark 5. This system uses passive sonobuoys which, when laid, transmit to a multichannel receiver in the aircraft the noises they hear. A computer then analyses the noises, for classification, by the Fast Fourier Transform (FFT) technique. This uses the ability of modern electronic circuitry to scan inputs very rapidly – several thousand times a second; and for a description of how the process sorts out the noise of a submarine from other ocean noises, the writer is indebted to *Jane's Weapon Systems* for the following, which he thinks even he understands: '... the constituent frequencies of a received signal, including randomly occurring noise, are separated so that the level (at each frequency) can be averaged over a short period of time, the whole process being repeated continuously and at a high rate . . . consistently-appearing signals are amplified with respect to noise, even though the latter may be far stronger at a given instant'. It need only be added that the signature thus obtained can be compared with known characteristics of allied and enemy submarines. FFT is, of course, used in passive equipments of all sorts these days but LAPADS has brought it into the helicopter field and its use is expected to increase.

Troop-Carrying Helicopters

The Sea King has, of course, a considerable load-carrying capacity in non-antisubmarine roles, typically 22 troops or 6,000lb (2,727kg) of cargo. A utility version, the Sea King HC Mark 4, of which 15 have been ordered, can carry up to 27 fully kitted troops or a 8,000lb (3,636kg) underslung load.

The main troop-carrying helicopter is still, however, the Wessex HU Mark 5. Powered by two 1,250 shaft horse power Rolls-Royce Gnome engines, this helicopter has a maximum take-off weight of 13,500lb (6,136kg); its rotor diameter is 56ft (16.98m). It can carry 14 fully-kitted troops, or an underslung Land Rover, from an off-lying commando carrier to shore. It can also pack an offensive punch, in the event of either small arms fire from the opposition during a landing or a requirement for support later on: it can carry 2-inch rockets on pods outside the undercarriage struts, or a fixed forward firing gun in the same position, or a SS 11 missile for anti-tank or anti-strong-point use. A general purpose machine gun can be fired through the side door.

Wessex HU5s are also used for search and rescue duties at the Royal Naval Air Stations, Portland, Culdrose, and Lee-on-Solent; and they form the VIP flight which is based at Lee-on-Solent.

Below left: The Sea King shows its versatility by lifting a 105mm light gun. *Crown Copyright*

Right: The Mark 4 troop-carrying version of the Westland Sea King. *Crown Copyright*

Below: Wessex 5 troop-carrying helicopters prepared to take off from the deck of a carrier. *Crown Copyright*

The Wessex 5 in various aspects of its role

Above: Landing in snowy terrain. *Crown Copyright*

Right: Firing air-to-ground rockets. *Crown Copyright*

Below right: Search and rescue. *Crown Copyright*

V/STOL Aircraft

The story of the development of the Hawker Siddeley Harrier, which has epic qualities, cannot be told here. It emerged in the middle 1960s as the only successful Western attempt to create a V/STOL aircraft with operational abilities, and was adopted for service in the close support role by the RAF with some misgivings, though the Army like the idea; 'I want' said an Army officer of my acquaintance, 'to be able to go out of my tent in the morning and pat it.' At that time the Royal Navy was reluctant to take on an aircraft which would cut across the well-established pattern of fixed-wing deck operations, and only when CVA-01 was cancelled did the Harrier come into the reckoning. Given an operating platform like the *Invincible* with no arrestor gear or catapults, or any other provision for operating high-performance fixed-wing aircraft, it gave the opportuniy for fixed-wing operations with all the advantages in time of conflict that have already been pointed out.

The Harrier's propulsion works on a simple principle. A single jet engine transmits its thrust through swivelling nozzles. When they point down, the aircraft goes up, or down in a controlled manner; when they point aft, it goes forward. Stability during vertical manoeuvres is provided by puffer-jets at the extremities of the aircraft. The technology that turns this principle into practice, in an effective fighting aircraft, is anything but simple, but is now well proven.

While it worked on exactly the same principles and used the technology, the Sea Harrier FRS Mark 1 – ordered in 1975 – needed to incorporate some modifications from the groundbased GR3. It has a more corrosion-resistant engine, the Pegasus 104 turbofan, and a raised cockpit for improved pilot vision. Its avionics include the Ferranti Blue Fox radar, which shares many characteristics with the Sea Spray and caters for air-to-air intercept and air-to-surface attack operations. A Head-up Display presents eye-level flight information to the pilot, relieving him of the need to peer into the cockpit. Navigational and communications equipment is of a high standard, and a radar warning receiver is built into the fin.

The Sea Harrier can carry a variety of armaments: Sidewinder heat-seeking missiles and an Aden gun for air-to-air missions, anti-surface ship missiles, bombs, rockets, flares and reconnaissance cameras. There are four points for such stores on the wings, the inboard ones having a maximum loading of over 3,000lb (1,365kg) each. The ski-jump will, of course, much increase the Sea Harrier's ability to get off the deck with an effective weapon and fuel load. Performance figures are, as

Below: A Sea Harrier of No 800 Squadron. *Crown Copyright*

Above left: Sea Harriers on operational trials in HMS *Hermes*. The aircraft ranged right aft, at the extreme right of the picture, carries a gun pack, Sidewinder missiles and long-range fuel tanks. *Crown Copyright*

Left: Sea Harrier with a full load airborne from HMS *Hermes*. *Crown Copyright*

Above: A Sea Harrier of No 800 Squadron makes the first deck landing on HMS *Invincible*. *Crown Copyright*

always, very dependent on these factors but speed in excess of Mach 0.8 in level flight, an intercept radius of 400 nautical miles and a ceiling of 40,000ft plus are published figures which indicate the fighting qualities of the aircraft.

The Sea Harrier is a lot longer than it is broad – wingspan is only 25ft 3¼in (7.70m) while length is 47ft 7in (14.50m) – so folding wings are foregone, but the Blue Fox folds back to port to improve ease of stowage.

By the early 1980s there will be three operational Sea Harrier squadrons: the headquarters squadron (899) at RNAS Yeovilton which is also the operational Flying Training unit, and two (800 and 801) nominated to HM Ships *Hermes* and *Invincible*.

The Royal Naval Air Stations

This chapter would not be complete without a brief description of the Royal Naval Air Stations ashore. However focussed on shipborne operations a fleet air arm may be – and the Royal Navy's could scarcely be more so – it needs a comprehensive shore organisation for training, administration and technical back-up.

HMS *Heron* at Yeovilton, Somerset, is now the centre of Fleet Air Arm activity. It is the headquarters of the Flag Officer, Naval Air Command, and is the parent station of Sea Harrier and troop-carrying helicopter squadrons. It is also the station at which the Lynx Intensive Flying Trials Unit formed and carried out its work. Currently all Lynx flights are parented here; after 1982, this function will move to RNAS Portland.

HMS *Seahawk* at Culdrose, Cornwall, is the parent station for Sea King anti-submarine helicopters and the training school for their pilots and for all observers. Intensive flying trials of new heavy anti-submarine helicopters have normally been conducted here, and the station has a very large search and rescue task, covering up to 200 miles out into the Atlantic.

The Royal Naval Air Station, Portland, which is part of HMS *Osprey*, is the parent station for Wasp ships' flights and provides helicopters also for a multitude of tasks connected with the Flag Officer, Sea Training's work-up organisation and for search and rescue. There will be further discussion of this in Chapter X.

HMS *Daedalus* at Lee-on-Solent and HMS *Gannet* at Prestwick, Scotland, are specialised small establishments, the former training air mechanics and operating search and rescue helicopters, the latter a squadron of Sea King helicopters working with submarines out of Faslane, and providing search and rescue cover for the west coast of Scotland.

The Future

From entry into squadron service to final phasing-out – often after extensive modifications and role-changes – most aircraft types last between 10 and 20 years. This is about half the life of a ship, and this discrepancy in turnround rates makes planning and prediction difficult, particularly as aircraft technology continues to move at a rapid rate. The relatively short life of aircraft also tends to overheat naval budgets: new can usually be much better, but it is a great deal more expensive. Nevertheless it is natural to pursue excellence, considering that the subsurface, surface and air threats with which the Fleet Air Arm must help to cope are so severe. The result will necessarily be a series of compromises, involving acceptance of the good lest the best should be financially out of the question, but rejecting the ineffective even if it is attractive and cheap.

In the small-ship anti-submarine helicopter field, the Lynx is only just in service and its potential for development is marked. Uprated engines are an evident pre-requisite for a large extension of role into, for example, anti-submarine localisation by sonobuoys. Micro-processing equipment on board this helicopter would be an important part of such a modification.

Large anti-submarine helicopters pose a more urgent problem. The Sea King HAS Mark 2 and Mark 5 are first-class machines, but many of the airframes have been in service 10 years already. Moreover, developments in the 1980s, including surface-ship towed-array passive sonars, the new Anglo-Australian Barra passive sonobuoys, the AQS 901 processing equipment, and improved active sonar are opening new horizons in the tactics of anti-submarine warfare. If they are to be fully exploited a helicopter of even better endurance, flexibility and processing capacity than the Sea King HAS Mark 5 is needed. The projected Anglo-Italian EH 101 would be such a helicopter.

New troop-carrying helicopters are almost certain to remain based on the Sea King, and if Sea Kings are replaced during the decade in the anti-submarine role some of the airframes thus released could be converted to the troop carrying role.

Finally, the Sea Harrier is, again, only just in service. But unlike the Lynx, it is a very developed aircraft; it is unlikely that this airframe can take much more in the way of avionics, weapon and extra thrust. A 'son of Harrier', either in the form of the US/UK AV 8B project or a big-wing, big-engine version, may turn out to be the answer. But no one will want to hurry into it until some experience has been gained of the Sea Harrier in squadron service at sea.

Perhaps one last word is necessary. It is noticeable, when one looks at the history of Fleet Air Arm types and equipment since before World War II, how many of the innovations and successes have started as private ventures. Some of these came from within the Fleet Air Arm itself as, for example, the brilliantly successful ideas of the angled deck, mirror landing sight, steam catapult and now the ski jump. Others were the brain-children of firms – not always the largest and most powerful. These innovations sometimes ran into doubt or opposition from the operational requirements staffs or the research and development establishments who, not unnaturally, preferred to pursue their own more evolutionary, and increasingly-expensive, ideas. The lesson is that, in the still very volatile technology of operations by shipborne aircraft, closed minds and NIH ('Not Invented Here – so it can't be any good') can not only delay the entry of useful equipment into service, they can cost a great deal of money. A receptive attitude, imagination and judgement on the part of staffs and scientists may be the best specific for the future health of the Fleet Air Arm. Of its operational professionalism and spirit there is no doubt.

Left: A formation of Gazelle helicopters from No 705 Squadron, RNAS Culdrose, where naval helicopter flying training is concentrated. Photo by FCPO Charles Robinson. *Crown Copyright*

6

The Royal Marines

The Royal Marines trace their history back to the raising of the Admiral's Regiment in 1664. In over three centuries of sea soldiering there are few things the Corps has not done and few places where it has not been. As early as the reign of George IV, so numerous were their battle honours that over 100 were cited to the King as worthy of inclusion on their colours; that monarch, with one of the happy short cuts of which he was sometimes capable, decreed the device of a globe surrounded with laurel, the motto 'Per mare per terram' and the single word 'Gibraltar': a commemoration of the matchless defence of 1704 and a symbol of rocklike steadiness under fire.

The fire has not always come from the enemy. The very variety and scope of the Royal Marines' activities, down the centuries, often led critics to suggest that they had no rational role either ashore or afloat, and that all their tasks could be better done by other organisations. The critics' logic might have seemed impeccable but was constantly confounded by the Marines' extraordinary effectiveness in everything they undertook. This, and a Corps spirit and cohesion unsurpassed by any military organisation anywhere, has ensured their survival today as a Corps of some 7,000 men.

The Commando Role

The commando idea evolved in World War II as a means of providing forces to spearhead attacks and secure lodgments for other forces to exploit. If there is a guiding principle of commando work, it is of special training to overcome every conceivable sort of obstacle. One obstacle is the enemy, of course; others may be the sea, rivers, cliffs, climatic conditions, and all these have defeated or frustrated military forces before now. In their special preparation to overcome all such obstacles, commando-trained forces are following the lead of the first commandos, those Boer farmers who made such formidable light forces in the war of 1900-1902.

It is entirely in keeping with the history of the Royal Marines, including their employment as commandos in World War II itself, that they should have inherited the responsibility for keeping the commando idea fully alive in all its versatility and adaptability. Moreover, Britain's concentration on NATO has

Below: Overcoming beach obstacles: Royal Marines making a landing from LCVPs in the Shetland Islands. *Crown Copyright*

Above: Overcoming climatic conditions: Royal Marines on an exercise in Northern Norway. *Crown Copyright*

not deprived commandos of their value; the vulnerable flanks of the Alliance, particularly in Norway, offer obstacles enough to challenge even highly trained and capable special troops.

Taking Northern Norway as a case in point, seven Russian divisions on the Finnmark border face Norwegian resident forces of not much more than brigade strength. The coastline is deeply indented, the terrain rocky, but the climate is the greatest natural obstacle: sub-zero temperatures and deep snow in winter, slush-mud- and mosquito-bearing daylight in summer. In such conditions, well-acclimatised and highly-trained light forces, introduced at an early enough stage to counter an aggression across the border, could be decisively effective in helping to delay and blunt its advance: decisively because other allied forces could arrive in strength, but – and this is the principal operational case for the special preparation of British forces — a good deal later.

There is, of course, a political case too. The flank countries of NATO happen to be the only ones that have a common border with the Soviet Union; this, and their remoteness from the heartland of the Central Front, tend to make them feel isolated and vulnerable. The prospect of timely support is the best Alliance cement there is. So long as potential opponents see NATO's meeting both the operational and political requirements, deterrence in this area can be expected to remain secure.

Organisation and Training

The Commandant-General of the Royal Marines, a lieutenant-general RM, has his headquarters in London and is backed by a small staff. Under him, the Royal Marines divide into two organisations each commanded by a major-general: MGRM Commando Forces, with his headquarters at Mount Wise in Plymouth, and MGRM Training and Reserve Forces, with his headquarters at Royal Marines Eastney, Portsmouth.

MGRM Commando Forces has command of 3 Commando Brigade Royal Marines, which as well as headquarters and a number of combat and logistic supporting units – of which more in a moment – consists of 40 Commando, based at Seaton Barracks, Plymouth; 42 Commando, at Bickleigh, Plymouth; and 45 Commando Group, at Arbroath, Scotland. 41 Commando has recently been disbanded and its men absorbed into other units.

Each Commando consists of about 650 Royal Marines under a lieutenant-colonel RM. Organisation is into companies and troops on orthodox infantry lines and infantry skills are the basis of the commandos' fighting qualities. The rifle companies hold weapons up to and including General Purpose Machine Guns (GPMG) and 2-inch mortars; the support company has a 81mm mortar troop, a MILAN anti-tank troop, an assault engineer troop, a sniper section and a reconnaissance troop. Basic vehicles and communications equipment are to normal infantry scales.

Special to the Royal Marines, however, are a number of skills and equipments. Most strikingly, the Brigade Headquarters, 45 Commando Group, 42 Commando and their supporting elements are equipped and trained for arctic warfare. They can ski, fight, and – more important than anything else – survive in the conditions expected in the Norwegian North and frequently exercise there. They are now equipped with Volvo BV 202 articulated over-snow vehicles, which are known as

Above: The BV 202 articulated over-snow vehicle lands in Northern Norway. *Crown Copyright*

Left: A Royal Naval Sea King helicopter lifts ashore a Gazelle belonging to 3 Commando Brigade Air Squadron. *Crown Copyright*

'Bandwagons'. Power is transmitted to the tracks of both components so that, as a colleague succinctly said, if the front can't pull the chances are that the back can push. The vehicle can also tow a light gun.

Under 3 Commando Brigade come a number of other units. Brigade Headquarters and the Commando Logistic Regiment are arctic warfare trained, so that a fully-supported two-commando arctic deployment is feasible. 59 Independent Commando Squadron of the Royal Engineers includes specialised vehicles for beachwork and bridging. 29 Commando Light Regiment, Royal Artillery, is fully integrated into Commando skills, as are the associated forward observers and forward air controllers who direct air support in operations. A raiding squadron attached to 3 Commando Brigade (the other two are at Poole and Hong Kong) operates both rigid and inflatable raiding craft, and the Brigade has its own helicopter squadron of Lynx and Gazelle aircraft.

Commando Forces also have a very close relationship with the Dutch Marines; 1 Amphibious Combat Group and W Independent Company of the Royal Netherlands Marine Corps form part of the UK/Netherlands Combined Landing Force, and the Dutch Marines are also fully trained and equipped for operations in Norway in winter. This fine Corps, with traditions as long and distinguished as those of the Royal Marines themselves, has thrown itself wholeheartedly into the business of

NATO flank support and makes a full contribution in skill and hardihood.

Incidentally, 45 Commando Group is referred to as a 'Group' because it is detached in Arbroath in Scotland with its own artillery battery, engineer troop, and flight of Gazelle helicopters, and it is joined for a large part of the year by W Company of the RNLMC with whom it has a very close affinity.

Also at Arbroath is the newly formed Comacchio Company, specially trained in tasks in connection with the protection from terrorist attack of our offshore gas and oil installations.

The MGRM (Training) has no less diverse responsibilities. Under him come the two main training centres of the Royal Marines, the Royal Marines School of Music, and the important administrative, secretariat and recruiting organisations which are run from Royal Marines Eastney. He is also responsible for the Royal Marines Reserve, all volunteers and numbering some 1,000 men.

The Commando Training Centre Royal Marines is at Lympstone, Devon. Here every Royal Marine recruit, except buglers and musicians, does a 32-week course in the full range of commando skills. Young officers do a year's training, including the full commando course. On completion of the course, and not before, a man can wear the green beret. He then generally joins a commando or headquarters unit, though some, such as clerks and cooks, go straight on to further training for their specialist tasks. There are departments for follow-up weapon training and for assault engineer training; training in heavier weapons takes place at Army establishments. At Lympstone, also, are run the NCOs' courses – junior for advancement to corporal, senior for promotion to sergeant, advanced for promotion to warrant officer. The Physical Training School is here too. Finally,

Lympstone is the centre of drill training in the Royal Marines under the corps adjutant and drill instructors. In all these areas of training the very highest standards are set.

The Amphibious Training Centre at Poole, Dorset, has three main functions. First, it trains landing craft personnel, who are volunteers from the rank of corporal upwards, in handling rigid and inflatable raiding craft, and large and small landing craft (LCVP and LCM, for initial-hunters). Second, it trains ships' Royal Marines detachments, which, in certain frigates on for example West Indies service, consist of about 10 men and in ships like *Fearless* and *Intrepid* are a good deal larger. This training is basically to accustom to sea life men whose previous experience has been largely land-based. Finally, ATC Poole trains a variety of craftsmen: motor transport drivers and mechanics, carpenters, metalsmiths, printers, equipment repairers. An offshoot of Poole, the Amphibious Trials and Training Unit at Instow, North Devon, carries out advanced work in the particularly suitable tidal and beach conditions there.

Right: Royal Marine Commandos on the flight deck of HMS *Hermes* **waiting to embark in a Sea King helicopter. The helicopter in the background is a Wessex Mark 5. (Photo by Danny du Feu).** *Crown Copyright*

Below: A Dutch landing craft in the dock of HMS *Fearless.* **The Royal Netherlands Marine Corps exercises frequently with the Royal Marines and RNLMC units are co-located with RM units for much of the year.** *Crown Copyright*

The Royal Marines School of Music at Deal trains buglers and musicians – there is a difference, since buglers, as the name implies, specialise in bugles and drums while musicians have a broader range of instruments – to the standard which is so well known to and appreciated by the general public.

This brief summary of Royal Marines organisation and activities has not been comprehensive. For example, no mention has been made of the Special Boat Section (SBS), which as the Royal Marines counterpart of the Special Air Service (SAS) shares the same levels of skills and the same need for reticence; nor of the close and necessary liaison with the Fleet Air Arm, in the form particularly of the two specialised troop-carrying helicopter squadrons 845 and 846. For these and all other omissions may we be forgiven; and move on to a brief account of a period in the recent history of the Royal Marines which, if it were not typical, would be remarkable as an illustration of the activities of the Corps. The chronology is taken from the Royal Marines' magazine *Globe and Laurel*.

Left: One end-product of Commando training; a Royal Marine climbs an ice-fall in Northern Norway. (Photo by 45 Commando photographic unit). *Crown Copyright*

Below: A more typical product of Commando training: highly professional infantry work in difficult conditions is shown by this well-camouflaged headquarters in the Outer Hebrides. *Crown Copyright*

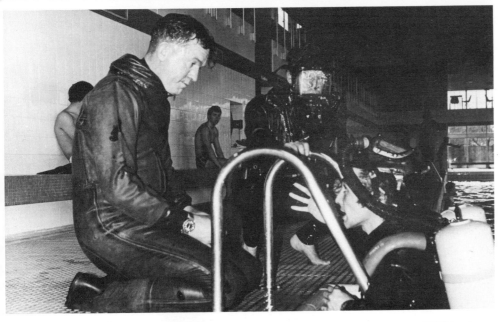

Above: Royal Marines of 'A' Company, 40 Commando, set up a Milan anti-tank weapon ambush during Exercise Teamwork 80. (Photo by Petty Officer P. Holgate). *Crown Copyright*

Left: Royal Marine Divers under training. *Crown Copyright*

Below Left: A Royal Marine canoeist brings his craft ashore during an exercise in Northern Norway. *Crown Copyright*

1979-80

The beginning of 1979 found all four Commandos in their home bases. None of them foresaw a restful year; in the event, some saw more movement than they had bargained for.

Within a couple of months 40 Commando was in Northern Ireland on a one-year resident posting, the first to be carried out by the Royal Marines and a helpful element in easing the stretch on Army units caused by frequent short deployments. 41 Commando was deployed on a mixture of public duties in London, jungle training in Brunei and acting as the Army's enemy in an exercise in Wales. 3 Commando Brigade Headquarters, 42 and 45 Commandos, the Commando Logistic Regiment and the bulk of the helicopters were in Norway, variously employed in the training and exercise deployments 'Clockwork' and 'Mainspring', folowed by the final exercise, more appropriately and explicitly called 'Cold Winter'. Meanwhile, the throughput of ships' detachments continued at Poole; and at the other end of the world, in the Falkland Islands, the 36 Royal Marines of Naval Party 8901 continued their lonely garrison.

By early summer there was another marked shift in the pattern. 42 and 45 were back from Norway and settling down to a summer of more general 'blackshod' training, including an exercise for 45 in Denmark, while 41 set off for an entirely new role: participation in the United Nations Force, Cyprus (UNFICYP) whose purpose is to keep the peace in the island and particularly in the buffer zone between the cease-fire lines that divide Greek and Turkish-occupied areas. Two Companies of the Commando were employed in UNFICYP while the other two garrisoned the Eastern Sovereign Base Area at Dhekelia; they rotated periodically. This tour was to be for six months and unaccompanied by wives and families, as this paricular tour – normally carried out by an Army unit – always is. Meanwhile, 40 Commando in Northern Ireland took over additional responsibility for patrolling County Fermanagh, the first infantry unit to do so; previously the task had fallen to resident armoured units.

Autumn brought its measure of the unexpected. The most tragic was the murder of Earl Mountbatten of Burma, the Life Colonel Commandant of the Corps. 45 Commando provided a guard of honour, marching party and street lining party for his funeral. But there were other calls as well. Illegal immigration into Hong Kong from the People's Republic of China had again reached a critical level and it was necessary to send 42 Commando to reinforce the hard-pressed units of the garrison that had been helping the civil authorities on and within the borders. Against a movement of population on this scale – of the order of 10,000 people a week – it was clearly impossible to catch everyone who tried to enter; the aim was to catch enough, and return them to China, to deter a mass movement; the stream must not be allowed to become a flood, for population pressure in Hong Kong was exceptionally high already. K Company was deployed in the marshes, L Company in the seaward approaches under Naval control, M Company (who three months earlier had been gracing the Royal Tournament) in paddy fields near the border. It was not particularly congenial work: the cheerful, dogged Chinese, spurred by economic pressures more than any other, were not enemies in any sense. Moreover, once returned they were quite likely to try again. But the job had to be done and 42 did it. It was typical of the year that, once home, they began pre-arctic training almost at once.

1980, too, brought its surprises. Agreement at the Lancaster House talks on Rhodesian independence resulted in the setting up – on the stroke of Christmas – of a Commonwealth Monitoring Force in which two teams of Royal Marines participated and served, as did everyone in that unique operation, with great credit. Arctic training by 42 and 45 went on as in 1979, 40 Commando came home from Northern Ireland and 41 prepared to go there on a shorter, but more operationally intense, tour. Nearer mid-year there were two shifts in the pattern, one scheduled and one unexpected. First, 45 donned their warm-weather clothing for the first time in many years for Exercise Dawn Patrol on NATO's Southern Flank; second, and with little warning, 42 found themselves, as Spearhead Battalion, at the other side of the world in the New Hebrides. They were needed there to help resolve a complex situation that had arisen in the run-up to independence. The plot may have seemed Gilbertian to onlookers but was touchy enough on the ground, and the presence of the Commando together with that of a detachment of French troops was enough to ensure the transition of the condominium into the new state of Vanuatu with an absolute minimum of bloodshed – sadly, there was one assassination a long way from any military presence.

Left: A demonstration of individual Commando skills. (Photo by Chief Petty Officer Drew). *Crown Copyright*

Below: A member of 40 Commando RM, and friends, in Belfast. *Crown Copyright*

The Future

It is easy enough, perhaps, to see in such an account a good many post-imperial as well as modern roles and draw the conclusion that the Royal Marines' task will diminish in future. There is another view that is more in accordance with history and, probably, a realistic prediction of what lies ahead. That is that highly adaptable troops, comprehensively trained and motivated to overcome obstacles whether they consist of an organised enemy or natural hazards or both, can exert an influence – whether deterrent or military – well beyond what might be expected from their numerical strength. Moreover, the Royal Marines are a natural outgrowth of this island nation. We have heard something of interfaces in earlier parts of this book; the Royal Marines live on yet another, between sea and shore. If they lose one role they will quite simply, and by merit, pick up another one in that area. Britain, and the world, have a lot of coastline.

Clearly the Royal Marines will have to contend with difficulties, of which the most severe will be the ageing and retirement of specialist amphibious shipping. But roll-on, roll-off and container ships increase in numbers all the time; so long as

Top: Royal Marines leaving a Sea King helicopter during an exercise in Arctic Norway. *Crown Copyright*

Above: Royal Marines of L Company, 42 Commando RM, boarding a junk off Hong Kong in search of illegal immigrants. (Photo by Petty Officer Eric G. Rooke). *Crown Copyright*

not too much money is spent on navalising them, they offer an option for cheap replacements. Helicopters, too, do not have to be custom-built for the amphibious role. The quality will reside principally in the men and in their training; and it is with a great deal of confidence that the survival of the Royal Marines can be predicted. Some years ago Major-General J. L. Moulton, Royal Marines, wrote: 'So versatile a Corps does not always fit tidily into the watertight compartments of departmental planning, but as history shows, no one can in reality foresee the type or hour of danger, or when the call will come again for a sheet anchor'. There is no need to add to those wise words.

7

The Offshore Tapestry

The phrase 'Offshore Tapestry' was coined in the early 1970s to describe the public management and good order of the sea areas round the United Kingdom in both peace and war. It aptly expresses the weaving of many strands that is necessary to ensure international order and national well-being. In the all too brief attempt to unravel them that follows, it is intended to move from preventive to curative measures, and from peace to war, so far as each strand of the tapestry allows.

The International Legal Position
International law already accords the United Kingdom sovereign rights for the exploration and exploitation of non-living, and certain living, resources of the sea bed and subsoil of the continental shelf round the United Kingdom. The definition in law of the outer limit of the shelf will probably settle eventually as nowhere less than 200 miles from the coast and in places a good deal further out. Living resources in the sea will almost certainly be the sovereign right of the UK out to 200 miles, but important modifications to this right will be imposed by the Common Fisheries Policy of the European Economic Community and by claims to historic rights of fishery by such countries as Poland and the USSR. The United Kingdom is likely to extend its territorial sea to 12 miles, preferably within the terms of a Law of the Sea Convention including satisfactory articles on freedom of navigation and overflight. In this belt it will have all the rights and responsibilities of sovereignty and may impose traffic, fiscal and pollution control regulations, while still recognising rights of innocent passage; in the belt out to 188 miles beyond, which it may then wish to designate as an Exclusive Economic Zone, its rights of regulation will be more limited and based on its sovereign rights over the resources, but it will clearly, in such a busily exploited and used sea area, have a profound interest in good order.

Hydrography
One of the very best bases for good order at sea is an accurate set of charts. Since its inception in 1795 the Hydrographic Department of the Royal Navy has set the highest standards; 'Trust in God and an Admiralty Chart' is still in the mariner's vocabulary. The Naval Surveying Service has, since the palm-fringed days when it charted the world, followed the general contraction of horizons, and most of its work is now done around the shores of the United Kingdom. There are good hydrographic, as well as political and economic, reasons for this. The North Sea and Channel are the busiest sea areas in the world, and the ones where deep-draught ships habitually work to the tightest depth margins. But depths here tend to be unstable; tides and gales cause phenomena such as sand waves, which can quickly and quite radically alter bottom contours. This demands a constant surveying effort. In more remote areas round our shores, the search for hitherto uncharted dangers still yields results; and today's remote area may become tomorrow's busy highway, in the quickly-moving technology of the sea. Finally, the emphasis on submarines in the modern Navy demands continuing ocean survey work, particularly in the Eastern Atlantic area.

To carry out these tasks the Hydrographer of the Navy has a fleet of 11 ships. While some are not in their first youth, they were designed and built to advanced technical standards and have proved capable of exceptionally swift and accurate work.

The ocean survey ships of the *Hecla* class are 260ft (78.9m) long and displace 2,800 tons. They have diesel-electric drive giving outstanding fuel economy and, with a bow thruster, flexible manoeuvring. There are electronic sensors of all sorts: high definition radar; Loran; Ship's Inertial Navigation System

Below: HMS *Hecla*, an ocean survey vessel. At the left of the picture is an ODAS (Ocean Data Acquisition System) buoy. *Crown Copyright*

Above right: Sextant and station pointer, still indispensable tools of the hydrographic surveyor's trade. Lieutenant-Commander (now Commander) Halliday at the Chart Table of HMS *Echo*. *Crown Copyright*

Right: A surveying recorder drawing a fair tracing of the day's sounding work. *Crown Copyright*

Below: HMS *Bulldog*, a coastal survey vessel. *Crown Copyright*

Above: A Royal Navy frigate standing by a stricken tanker presenting a pollution hazard. *Crown Copyright*

(SINS); satellite navigation; the HIFIX-6 Decca position-finding system which works by measuring phase difference between synchronised signals from a master station in the ship and slave stations ashore; echo-sounders both in the ship and her two surveying motorboats; instruments for collecting sediment, bottom core and water samples; a gravimeter and magnetometer; and a towed sidescan sonar that covers an area 300 metres either side of the ship's track. Data is fed in to three main processing areas: the automatic plotter on which the ship's position is constantly recorded together with other chosen data, the dry laboratory where the ship's main computer carries out calculating and recording functions, and the wet laboratory where the properties of the sea samples are analysed.

The coastal survey vessels are not oceanographic craft. They do not, therefore, have laboratories nor the comprehensive sampling facilities of the ocean survey ships. This apart, they are capable of an equally sophisticated surveying effort. They too have HIFIX-6, side and ahead scanning sonars, and two surveying motorboats for inshore and harbour surveying work. Finally, the inshore survey craft, converted from inshore minesweepers, are capable of work in estuaries and close offshore to the same standards of accuracy as their larger counterparts.

Surveying ships' crews range from about 120 in the *Hecla* class to some 20 in the Inshore Survey craft. When the ship is on survey work, everyone is involved, detachments on inshore work, coastlining or setting up fixing aids are frequent, and the work is as varied and absorbing as anything else the Navy can offer.

Traffic Regulation

Schemes for the separation of shipping traffic into lanes for travel in a certain direction are comparatively recent in their origin. In general, their mandatory nature stems not from the state off whose coast they lie – though states are allowed to make schemes within their territorial sea compulsory under municipal law – but from the agreement of ships' flag states. Consequently the enforcement of such schemes is generally a matter of informing and warning, rather than directing or arresting transgressors. The Royal Navy has a general responsibility for the information and warning function if it is appropriate, but it generally falls to other agencies – such as, in the case of the Dover Strait scheme, HM Coastguard through its radar and radio station at St Margaret's Bay – and no naval forces are specifically provided for it, though surface ship and air surveillance has been conducted from time to time.

Buoyage, Wreck Marking and Salvage

No less than traffic regulation, these are essential elements of good order in coastal waters. The first two are, in British waters outside port limits, the responsibility of Trinity House. The last is an area of tangled commercial and legal brambles into which the writer is reluctant to burrow, except to say that if a machete is not soon taken to it, shipping and insurance interests will only have themselves to blame when coastal states claim the right to intervene after a marine casualty.

Customs and Excise

The British Customs and Excise run their own water craft, and the Royal Navy exercises no jurisdiction in such matters except in the unlikely case of resistance to or assault on customs officers or their vessels.

Pollution Control

Control of maritime pollution is the responsibility of the Department of Trade. Vessel-source pollution accounts for about a quarter of all marine pollution, and its control falls into three categories: first, the prevention of collisions and groundings (traffic regulation, buoyage and navigational aids, and scrutiny in port of ships' equipment and standards of competence all help here); second, the containment of pollution after a casualty; and finally, the prevention of deliberate discharges of pollutants.

The Royal Navy's task in this area is, if not exactly incidental, hard to define. It does not conduct standing anti-pollution patrols, for which ships, which cannot view a large area of sea, are unsuitable anyway. On the other hand, if pollution is reported by some other agency – it will more often than not be an aircraft – closer investigation may well be assigned to the Navy, and in cases where international law allows an arrest, that will be the Navy's job too. Finally, marine casualties, and particularly those that cause pollution, almost invariably require Naval presence to provide on-the-spot information and control.

Fishery Protection

Firmly in the Navy's province, however, is the task of Fishery Protection. The Fishery Protection Squadron claims, indeed, to have the oldest job in the Navy, dating back to 1379. It may have been simpler then. It is certainly very complicated now, with fishing rights in dispute and various means of relieving the hard-pressed fish stocks — such as catch quotas, close seasons, closed areas, minimum net sizes and licences — more or less generally agreed among the participants in the very busy fisheries around the United Kingdom.

For many years fishery protection was carried out by ships designed for other tasks: frigates whose prime role was anti-submarine work, and coastal minesweepers. Only recently has the Royal Navy provided specialised patrol craft for offshore duties.

The *Island* class offshore patrol vessels, which came into service between 1977 and 1979, are 195ft (52.2m) long and of 1,000 tons standard displacement. They are trawler-shaped and stabilisers have improved their seakeeping. Two diesel engines, driving a single shaft, give them 16 knots. They will shortly be joined by

Below: An offshore patrol vessel, HMS *Guernsey*, flying the Fishery Protection flag. *Crown Copyright*

Right: HMS *Jersey* on patrol near an oil rig in the North Sea. *Crown Copyright*

Below right: A Naval fireman fighting a blaze on board a merchant vessel off the coast of Scotland. (Photo by Leading Airman H. Davison. The name of the fireman, from HMS *Hydra*, was unfortunately not recorded). *Crown Copyright*

the first of the *Castle* class, 264ft long and twin-screw, which as well as having the better seakeeping that greater length gives, will be able to land on and fuel a Sea King helicopter. So large, indeed, are offshore patrol vessels becoming that it is tempting to think of them as corvettes. But of course their armament (one 40mm Bofors) and crew (40-50) quickly belie that suggestion.

As these vessels come into service, the coastal minesweepers still in the Fishery Protection Squadron are likely to be retired or take up roles closer inshore. But they have done sterling work, and many of their exploits in keeping control of fisheries while using the minimum of force will long be remembered, from the countless crossings in bucketing Gemini dinghies to trawlers for net inspection, to a famous occasion when a minesweeper ran alongside a poaching trawler at dead of night with Wagnerian menace, furiously firing blank Bofors on the disengaged bow and assaulting the trawler's bridge window with a single well-directed King Edward potato. Surrender was instantaneous.

Oil and Gas Rig Protection

The threat to oil and gas installations in the North Sea has been a matter of debate since the early 1970s. Views on it have ranged from highly alarmist, which sees saboteurs clinging to the legs of every rig, to totally complacent. Whatever view is taken – and so important is the resource that the complacent extreme must be foolhardy – the chief deterrent must lie in random patrols by watchful and capable units both above and under the surface, and a quick-reaction force that can respond if a threat is found to develop.

Above-water patrols are the responsibility mainly of the Fishery Protection Squadron, some units of which may have in consequence to be deployed in areas of less than maximum efficiency for their fishery task. Underwater surveillance is, of course, often conducted by the oil companies themselves but Royal Navy divers have exercised from time to time on the rigs. A new Seabed Operations Vessel, HMS *Challenger*, has recently been launched. Finally, quick reaction to a developed threat is provided by Comacchio Company of the Royal Marines, 400 strong and stationed at Arbroath. Specially trained in rig protection work, using helicopters or raiding craft as appropriate, they would make any would-be hi-jacker or saboteur think several times. Quick reaction of another kind could come from a hydrofoil craft; the Boeing jetfoil HMS *Speedy* is under evaluation.

Above left: Rescue from the Danish coaster *Mere Enterprise* off Devon, 1974. Altogether five Sea King helicopters took part in this operation which rescued seven people. Two of the Sea Kings belonged to the Federal German Navy based at Culdrose.(Photo by Leading Airman S. Collinson). *Crown Copyright*

Left: A Sea King helicopter from Royal Naval Air Station, Prestwick, transferring an injured crew member from the Barra Island lifeboat during assistance operations for MV *Sapphire*, 1979. (Photo by Dave Cutler). *Crown Copyright*

Above: HMS *Abdiel*, a 1500 ton exercise minelayer and headquarters ship for minesweeping squadrons. *Crown Copyright*

Life-saving
In the event of marine casualties round the British coast, a variety of agencies may be involved in lifesaving: the Royal National Lifeboat Institution, HM Coastguard, British or foreign merchant ships, RAF aircraft, or ships and aircraft of the RN. Naval helicopters specifically for lifesaving purposes are kept at the Royal Naval Air Stations, Culdrose and Lee-on-Solent; some helicopters at Portland and Prestwick also have a search and rescue role. The statistics in the 1980 Statement on the Defence Estimates show that there was little standing and waiting, and a lot of action: in 1979 naval helicopters were called out 407 times, and assisted 313 people.

A further function of the Royal Navy in search and rescue operations is to provide command and control from maritime headquarters when required. Overall responsibilty for search and rescue, however, rests with the Department of Trade.

Mine Countermeasures
So this summary finally reaches a war task: although mine countermeasures are not, on current definitions, part of the Offshore Tapestry, it is convenient to include them here. While NATO recognises the importance of the sea approaches to its harbours, the clearance of mines is a national task. In the early 1950s the United Kingdom, spurred by the experience of the Korean war, made provision for mine countermeasures by building many coastal minesweepers, but their numbers have now dwindled to about 30.

The threat itself has not dwindled. Soviet mine stocks are enormous and most of their submarines and aircraft are capable of laying mines. All the known arming techniques – contact by the hull of a ship, the magnetic influence of a ship's hull, the noise of its engines, and the pressure waves it creates – are available in Soviet mines, as are devices such as ship-count which allows several ships to pass unscathed and then goes off under the next unsuspecting passer-by.

Each of these arming techniques requires a different form of sweeping and, moreover, it is necessary that the minesweeper should have very low magnetic and acoustic signatures so that it will not itself set off a mine before the sweeping gear passes over it. In shallow water, indeed, it is possible for the ship to search ahead of itself with a high-definition sonar and, if it detects an object that may be a mine, to stop, investigate and if necessary

Left: HMS *Bronington*, a coastal minesweeper converted to minehunting. Such ships are not confined to that task; in this picture *Bronington*, with HRH the Prince of Wales in command, was shadowing a Soviet submarine in the Channel. *Crown Copyright*

Below left: HMS *Soberton*, a coastal minesweeper, seen here on fishery protection duties. *Crown Copyright*

Right: Acoustic minesweeping: the minesweeper tows the Osborn Towed Acoustic Generator (TAG), the cylindrical device on the left, which generates wideband sound. The Towed Acoustic Monitor, the 'winged' body at the end of the other wire, listens to the sound actually transmitted by the TAG so that the ship can, if desired, adjust it to suit varying water conditions. Magnetic and moored mine actuation systems require different methods of sweeping. All require quiet, non-magnetic, manoeuvrable, expensive minesweepers. *Sketch: Sperry Gyroscope*

Below: HMS *Brecon*, first of the Hunt class Mine Countermeasures vessels, equipped for both sweeping and hunting. *Crown Copyright*

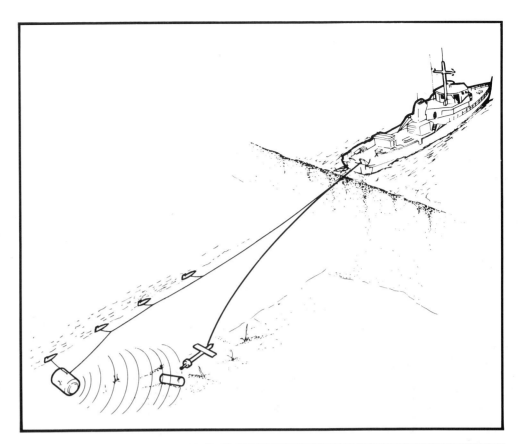

destroy it. This latter technique is called minehunting, and about half the coastal minesweepers were converted to it.

In practice both sweeping and hunting methods are needed, and the Royal Navy's solution in its new Hunt class mine countermeasures vessels is to combine all the capabilities in one hull. This is particularly important for the Clyde approaches. But it means a large and expensive ship. Hunt class vessels are 197ft (60m) long, of 615 tons standard displacement. They have two Ruston Paxman Deltic diesel engines, with a further unit for the slow-speed drive needed in hunting and bow thruster for manoeuvrability. Sweeping gear includes the Sperry Osborn acoustic towed body, the magnetic MM 11 loop and the wire Oropesa Mark 3 Mod 2 to cut the cables of moored mines. Hunting gear includes the well-tried Type 193 M sonar and the French PAP-104 investigation and destruction vehicle, in effect a small, unmanned, television-equipped, remotely-controlled

submarine. Navigation gear, most important in minesweeping and hunting, is very advanced and includes HIFIX-6. But the most striking fact about the Hunt class is that their hulls are of glass reinforced plastic, non-magnetic and strong but requiring very advanced construction techniques.

While no doubt the Royal Navy would like a large number of such ships, their cost is high and it will have to make do with something simpler for the clearance of East Coast port approaches. This will be a specialised hunter; various designs, British and foreign, exist. There are also plans for coping with a particular menace, the deep-laid rising mine, by the use of deep-sweeping trawlers. Finally, the hovercraft as a mine countermeasures vehicle is still under evaluation. It has many advantages, including low signatures and remarkable resistance to underwater explosions, but its rather poor towing ability and navigational imprecision are against it.

Port Organisation and Defence

In time of tension or war, it would be necessary to provide defence for the ports of the United Kingdom and bring under naval control the shipping that uses them. This task would fall mainly to the Royal Naval Reserve and the Royal Naval Auxiliary Service, with some backing from regular officers and ratings either serving or recalled to service. Naval Control of Shipping is regularly exercised, so that training, adaptability and dedication can be expected to make the best use of the limited resources that are maintained in peacetime for Naval Control of Shipping and port defence.

The Future

The Offshore Tapestry is a design that can change quite fast. Ten years ago there were no offshore patrol vessels even on the drawing board. Continued development of Britain's offshore estate, the declaration of an Exclusive Economic Zone, Common Market and environmentalist pressures, may all add impetus to movement that is already going on. Nor will the mine threat go away. The trend to specialisation of craft, which has already led to four or five types replacing – albeit with more effectiveness – the ubiquitous coastal minesweeper, may well continue and add to the resources spent on the Offshore Tapestry.

What proportion of those resources should come from the Navy's budget is likely to remain controversial. Surveying, offshore patrol and protection, surveillance for traffic safety and pollution control are arguably not defence tasks. In the way in which responsibilities for them have evolved, however, many of them have fallen to the Royal Navy; and it seems unlikely that any radical reorganisation, for example on the lines of the United States Coastguard, will occur to change that. It is therefore to be hoped that inter-departmental financial arrangements will result in realistic provision for what is a very real national task.

Below: Under evaluation: the jetfoil HMS *Speedy. Crown Copyright*

8

Fleet Support

A complex and highly technical organisation like the Royal Navy requires, by its nature, comprehensive stores and maintenance back-up to keep it at readiness. Even in the days of Pepys, it was very difficult to provide fleet support directly from private or commercial sources. It is many times more so now, and the Navy has perforce to run its own support organisation. That organisation costs, at 1980 prices, about £1,000m a year to run: the turnover of a very large firm indeed.

It is, consequently, not possible in a few thousand words to explain in detail how the support of the Fleet is organised and run. There will be many short cuts in what follows, and experts will find, no doubt, some inaccuracies of emphasis if not of fact.

Support can be thought of as a flow of material and skills, moving towards a final destination in the Fleet's ships, aircraft and men. It is a largely civilian affair in its earlier stages, and sometimes stays in civilian channels for most of its course. This being so, it is not entirely surprising that over 60,000 civilians are employed in Fleet support: that is, very nearly one for every uniformed member of the naval Service. The flow of support can be divided into two main streams: stores, provisions and fuel; and maintenance, repair and refit.

Stores, Provisions and Fuel

Initial procurement and holding of naval stores, of which there are 834,000 separate inventory items, of armament and victualling stores and fuel, are the responsibility of the Royal Naval Supply and Transport Service (RNSTS) under its director-general, a civilian of roughly equivalent rank to a rear-admiral, who is responsible in turn to the Chief of Fleet Support, a vice-admiral or admiral and a member of the Admiralty Board.

Apart from headquarters staff, the RNSTS has a considerable number of departments and depots round the country. These are not, as might be expected, grouped closely round the naval ports of Portsmouth, Devonport, Chatham, Rosyth and Faslane, although of course there are stores departments at all those places, and some stores and most victualling depots do tend to be close by. But the hardware, armament and fuel depots are pretty widely scattered due to a combination of history (that was where

Below: Handling stores in a Royal Fleet Auxiliary. The naval stores inventory runs to over 800,000 separate categories. *Crown Copyright*

they finished World War II, and new real-estate, to say nothing of new buildings and plant, is hard to come by) and policy (dispersal is helpful in terms both of defence against sabotage, and in bringing employment to places that need it).

Thus there are for example Royal Naval Stores Depots at Exeter, Deptford, Slough, Eaglescliffe in Northumberland and Llangennech in Wales; Armament Depots at Dean Hill and Broughton Moor in England, Trecwn in Wales, Beith and Coulport in Scotland; Fuel Depots at Invergordon, Falmouth and the Isle of Grain. Overseas, fuel is held at several locations such as Gibraltar, Singapore and the Falkland Islands. The United Kingdom participates in many NATO logistic infrastructure projects, some of them in Britain like the NATO fuel depots in Cambeltown and Loch Ewe, some in the Mediterranean.

Computers are extensively used for stock control. Central control of stocking and procurement is carried out at Bath, certain categories of items are subject to functional stock control at depots – for example, electronic material at Copenacre and machinery spare parts at Eaglescliffe – and local holdings at naval bases are also subject to computer control. These measures have alleviated, though they can never entirely cure, the problem of the vital bit that is not where it is needed; they are also a safeguard against overstocking.

When stores arrive on board ship or shore establishment they are taken on charge by the naval personnel of the Supply Department concerned and issued to users as they are required.

Top left: **A Wren stores accountant. Computers are extensively used in the Royal Navy's stores operations.** *Crown Copyright*

Left: **The RFA tanker** *Gold Rover* **at Portland. Other units in the picture include a Lynx helicopter, a County class destroyer and a Ness class storeship. (Photo by Leading Airman Schwartz).** *Crown Copyright*

Top right: **RFA** *Olwen*, **a large fleet tanker with six abeam fuelling points and a helicopter flight deck and hangar.** *Crown Copyright*

Above: **The RFA support tanker** *Appleleaf*. *Crown Copyright*

Some computer assistance is used here too, and it can be expected that ships' stores departments will make increasing use of this tool.

In general, ships' main stores and ammunition requirements are supplied in harbour. But in time of tension or war it would be operationally crippling to rely on harbour supply, and in consequence the Royal Navy has full facilities, frequently exercised in peacetime, for the supply at sea of all kinds of stores, provisions and fuel. This supply is in the hands of the Royal Fleet Auxiliary (RFA).

The Royal Fleet Auxiliary

The ships of the RFA, numbering at present 26 hulls with a total gross registered tonnage in excess of 300,000, occupy an unusual position in international law. They are government ships on non-commercial service, and thus enjoy many of the immunities that warships do; but, being non-combatants and civilian-manned, they have many of the freedoms that merchant ships can claim, such as unannounced entry into foreign ports. They fly the blue ensign, and the officers and many of the men regard the RFA as a lifetime career.

Because fuel, in any conventionally powered warship, is used up much more quickly at sea than solid stores, the tanker element of the RFA has to be numerous and widely deployed. Tankers are of three kinds: large and small fleet tankers, whose main job is replenishment at sea, and support tankers which are mainly employed in freighting naval oil supplies in bulk.

There are five large fleet tankers at present operating. All came into service between 1963 and 1966. *Olna*, *Olmeda* and *Olwen* are some 650ft (198m) long, of 25,000 tons deadweight and powered by double-reduction geared turbines of 26,500 shaft horsepower making them capable of 19 knots. *Tidespring* and *Tidepool* are rather smaller all round and a knot slower. Crews hover around the 100 mark. The most distinctive features of these ships are their gantries and derricks amidships which carry the underway refuelling gear, and their flight decks and hangars aft which can accommodate up to three Sea King helicopters.

The small Fleet Tankers are of the *Rover* class – *Green*, *Grey*, *Blue*, *Gold* and *Black*. 460ft (140.6m) long, they are of 6,700 tons deadweight and diesel-powered, but can even so do 19 knots. They carry limited dry cargo and refrigerated stores and have a helicopter deck aft, but no hangar.

Fuelling at sea is a routine operation for both RFAs and warships, taking place during a protracted exercise or deployment once every three or four days. However routine it may be, it demands care. It entails the warship's steaming parallel to the tanker at a distance of about 100 feet, usually for a period of over an hour. Since the passage of a ship through the water generates zones of pressure at the bow and stern, and of suction amidships, the approach to and disengagement from this close station are times requiring particular alertness. So, of course, are they the moments at which modern-day seamanship comes into its own, as first lieutenants, engineer officers and their men strive to reduce to a minimum the dead time between the moment the first line, fired by a line-throwing rifle, goes across and the connection of the hose and beginning of pumping by the tanker. The heavy rubber hose is supported by troughs hung from the tanker's derrick and by a hanging-off pendant attached to a strong point in the receiving ship. Apart from a distance line, marked every 20 feet and stretched between the ships as a handy means of indicating the current distance between them, and a telephone line for communication between bridges and fuelling points, the hose with its attendant wire is the only physical connection between the two ships during refuelling.

Right: Abeam fuelling. The hose to HMS *Argonaut* (right of picture) is connected, while that to HMS *London* (left of picture) has just been disconnected. The tanker is RFA *Olna*. *Crown Copyright*

Below: Abeam fuelling. A close-up view of derrick, hose and trough arrangements. *Crown Copyright*

The support tankers of the *Leaf* class, at present four commercial tankers of 20-30,000 tons deadweight on charter, have been modified to allow limited replenishment at sea, but generally are occupied in freighting.

The second large category of RFAs is the fleet replenishment ships, which supply solid stores. Newest are the *Fort Grange* and *Fort Austin*, in service in 1978-9. 603ft (184.4m) long, with a full load tonnage of 23,600, they are diesel-powered and can do 21 knots. Ten years older but of similar dimensions are the *Resource* and *Regent*; their steam turbines give them one knot less. All these four ships carry armament as well as victualling and naval stores. Future ships are planned to have oil fuel for transfer as well, thus attaining the ideal of the 'one-stop ship' and simplifying further the operational problems of resupply at sea. More limited, because she does not carry armament stores, is the *Stromness*, a ship of 16,792 tons built in 1967. As in the larger replenishment ships, extensive use is made of palletised loads, powered roller transporters and other cargo handling aids. Closed circuit television is used to control cargo flow.

All the solids replenishment ships carry complements drawn both from the RFA and the RNSTS, since of course stores holding and issue is much more complex than in the case of fuel. Total crews range from 130 to 250.

Solids replenishment at sea generates a ship-handling and station-keeping problem similar to that of fuelling, except that the heavy jackstay gear used demands that distances apart are even smaller. The wire jackstay, hauled across and secured in the receiving ship, is kept taut by a self-tensioning winch in the RFA and forms a high-wire across which a traveller carrying the stores can be hauled back and forth. One of the most difficult problems in the receiving ship is moving the stores quickly away from the reception point without denting the deck, the upperworks, the stores themselves, or the sailors moving them.

Transfers of small amounts of solids can, of course, be carried out by helicopter; there is no need for it to settle on the deck of the receiving ship, it can merely winch the stores down. This method adds a flexibility and speed to the whole replenishment-at-sea pattern which, in operational circumstances, might prove vital, since replenishment is a tactically somewhat vulnerable time. The other way in which the helicopter holdings of RFAs may prove of tactical importance is, of course, their value as anti-submarine units – either operating from the RFA under the control of the replenishment group's screen commander, or flown to a large warship as reinforcement or replacement for lost or unserviceable aircraft.

One RFA, indeed, exists entirely as a helicopter carrier, for training and spare-deck duties. This is the *Engadine*, normally based at Portland. Another part of the RFA consists of the six Landing Ships (Logistic), with Arthurian names, which are run mainly on behalf of the Army.

Top left: The fleet replenishment ship *Fort Austin* **with Sea King helicopters on both flight decks.** *Crown Copyright*

Above left: RFA *Regent,* **a large fleet replenishment ship built in 1968.** *Crown Copyright*

Above: Replenishment with solid stores by heavy jackstay. HMS *Bristol* **receives a palletised load from a storeship.** *Crown Copyright*

Right: A naval helicopter pilot and a RFA officer confer over the chart in the helicopter support ship *Engadine. Crown Copyright*

Refit, Repair and Maintenance

The 'heavy end' of the Royal Navy's refit and repair organisation is provided by the Royal Dockyards at Portsmouth, Devonport, Chatham and Rosyth, with HM Dockyard at Gibraltar and the Naval Bases, Faslane and Portland also playing an important part. At all these places the main workforce is civilian, and it totals at present over 36,000. The range of crafts and skills is very wide indeed. All the major dockyards run their own training centres, at which in 1979 nearly 4,000 apprentices were under training.

The term 'normal refit' is applied to the prolonged period in dockyard hands during which defects are rectified and alterations and additions undertaken. Modernisations, which generally occur at the mid-life of the major surface vessel classes, are called 'major refits'; some of these may last for two years, even more in the case of ships that require restorative hull work. The period between refits has tended to increase as more reliance has been placed on maintenance based on observed performance, and on repair of equipment by exchange; also the advent of gas turbines has enabled engine changes to be done without the ship's being taken in hand in a dockyard. Between refits a ship has scheduled periods with help from the Fleet Maintenance Units, which are teams of Naval personnel who augment the ship's company in order to help with essential defects and planned maintenance work. While these teams generally join up with ships when they are in the naval bases at home, they may go further afield; during Fleet deployments, for example, they have flown to Sydney or Singapore to take part in ships' assisted maintenance periods.

Over the last decade the dockyards have suffered from the same problems as much of the rest of British industry. These difficulties have been compounded by the extremely complex organisational problem of catering, ship by ship, for a stream of defects no two of which are precisely alike. However standardised equipment may have become within classes, and however much repair-by-replacement is the standard method dealing with an ever wider series of circumstances, there will always be aspects of uniqueness whenever a ship comes in for attention. The defect list which is rendered before arrival will do its best to describe what is wrong, but only investigation will reveal the full extent of each fault and problem.

In many ways the running of a peacetime dockyard organisation, with the need to turn out finished work to exact specifications, is more difficult than carrying out battle repairs which have to be quick but do not have to be standard. The dockyards must, of course, keep the latter art alive.

Recent facilities added to the Royal Dockyards have given them capabilities which match those in the best repair yards in the world. Among these are the facilities for refitting nuclear-powered submarines in Devonport, Rosyth and Chatham, the covered frigate complex at Devonport and the synchrolift at Rosyth. With their proud traditions and skills, the Royal Dockyards continue to provide a loyal service to the Fleet.

The naval bases in which the dockyards are situated are also the home ports for the majority of Her Majesty's ships. This means that they operate a large number of auxiliary craft to provide harbour services: these belong to the Royal Maritime Auxiliary

Above left: A Scorpion armoured reconnaissance vehicle is embarked in the logistic landing ship *Sir Galahad. Crown Copyright*

Above: The synchrolift at Rosyth: a modern and economical alternative to dry-docking for small vessels. *Crown Copyright*

Right: The RMAS mooring, salvage and boom vessel *Goosander*, **one of over 600 craft of various types and purposes that support the fighting fleet.** *Crown Copyright*

service, and are civilian-manned. No less than 664 of them were listed in November 1979, and even when 200 harbour launches and 225 dumb lighters are taken into account they still make up an impressive array. There are mooring craft, waterboats, fuel carriers, vessels connected with diving and underwater trials of all sorts; and finally, five ocean tugs and 44 harbour tugs.

The Royal Navy also runs the helicopter repair organisation for all three fighting Services. This is based at the Royal Naval Aircraft Yards at Fleetlands and Wroughton. The total number of rotary-wing aircraft supported is nearly 900, and of these up to 200 pass through the RNAYs each year. Engine overhauls total more than 300 a year; these are done at Fleetlands only.

Below: The submarine refitting complex at Devonport. *Crown Copyright*

Bottom: The covered frigate complex at HM Naval Base, Devonport. *Crown Copyright*

The Future

The Fleet support requirement has to take account of two major pressures which, unfortunately, are in opposing directions. One is the increasing complexity of modern units; the other is the need for economy. Plans for the next 10 years emphasise the need to cut costs. Thus, on the projections announced in June 1981, the Royal Dockyard at Chatham will close in 1984, there will be a sharp reduction in dockyard work at Portsmouth (though naval base facilities will be retained), and consideration is being given, in consultation with the Gibraltar Government, to the future of the Gibraltar yard. Several stores depots will be closed, and Royal Fleet auxiliary numbers will be somewhat reduced. These changes are the corollary of the reduction in ship refits and, particularly, mid-life modernisations, as well as the overall reduction in destroyer and frigate numbers, which were outlined in Chapter IV. During the decade a drive can be expected in the direction, as the White Paper has it, of 'tauter and more accountable management and improvements in efficiency'. We can all wish that well; but, as this Chapter has suggested, the task of support is no easy one, ashore or afloat. It has been with us since well before the days of Samuel Pepys, and it will not go away now.

9

The Women's Royal Naval Service

Women first served with the Royal Navy in 1917, when the Women's Royal Naval Service was formed under its first Commandant, Dame Katherine Furse, and with an aim succinctly expressed as 'free a man to fight'. It reached a strength of 7,000 by the end of the war, but its achievements – which were remarkable and many – did not save it from being disbanded in 1919. Only when a similar emergency threatened in 1939 was it reconstituted. At the end of World War II it totalled 74,600 women, and this time its value was so indisputable that it remained in being, and in 1949 was established as a permanent and integral part of the Royal Navy. Peacetime numbers, however, fell to less than a tenth of the wartime maximum – a factor which, by the way, emerges again and again as a common statistic of the Navy's war-to-peace transition.

Neither during the wars nor subsequently did the WRNS serve in warships. For many years they did not come under the Naval Discipline Act, and this emphasised the voluntary basis of their service and gave them a somewhat special position in the establishments in which they served. This was reflected in the organisation of such establishments; the WRNS unit was an entity, under a WRNS officer, exerting its own discipline and administration though, of course, making use of and contributing to the common services of the establishment.

While this gave a strong and welcome identity to the Service, it had some disadvantages too. Many officers were occupied entirely in administration, when they had other skills to offer which would have helped the Navy's work; and girls could in theory (and some did) quit the Service without notice, leaving important complement billets unfilled. From the early 1970s, therefore, the WRNS began to look for a more integrated role within the naval service, though still as a separate service wearing its distinctive uniform. A study group was formed and reported in 1974, and thereafter the WRNS moved steadily in the direction of integration.

In 1975, the appointing and drafting of WRNS officers and ratings passed to the naval organisations which already dealt with the male side of the service. In 1976, officers' training – previously at Greenwich – moved to the Royal Naval College, Dartmouth. In 1977 came the change that raised more eyebrows than any other: the WRNS came under the Naval Discipline Act. (There were one or two saving clauses; for example, a Wren can be placed in cells only for her own protection). The disciplinary effect, in a service which had long taken a pride in its self-discipline, was negligible, but a spin-off in terms of administrative officers released for other tasks was considerable, and led to a much closer lining-up of WRNS and RN specialisations with, of course, the prospect of many billets becoming available for either male or female incumbents. This was followed, in later years, by a closer alignment of career patterns and of rating structure.

Officer Structure

It is possible to become a WRNS officer by one of three routes: Direct Entry, whereby a graduate of between 20½ and 26, having passed the Admiralty Interview Board, does new entry training as a wren at HMS *Dauntless* followed by two months service at a Naval establishment to gain experience of the Navy and its organisation before joining the Royal Naval College, Dartmouth for officer training; Cadet Entry, where a girl of 18½ to 25 with five 'O' and two 'A' levels joins as a rating but with the assurance that within 15 months she will attend the Admiralty Interview Board and go on to officer training if she passes; and Rating

Left: Admiral Sir Desmond Cassidi, Second Sea Lord and Chief of Naval Personnel, inspects a passing-out parade at HMS *Dauntless*, the WRNS training establishment. *Crown Copyright*

Entry, where a girl of between 19½ and 25 who entered as a WRNS rating is recommended, if she shows potential and has five GCE passes, to attend the Admiralty Interview Board and on successful completion of this goes on to the officers' training course. On promotion to WRNS officer, all entrants are appointed to an eight-year short career commission, with options of extension to longer, pensionable careers after five years' service.

The jobs that WRNS officers do in naval establishments are so varied, and are in such a rapid state of development, that it is possible only to indicate broad categories and groups. Later in this chapter it will be possible to trace the trend for the future.

The supply and secretarial group is perhaps that most closely integrated at present with its male counterpart. WRNS officers carry out the duties of secretary to commanding and senior officers, catering and mess management, and pay and cash charge and accounting. Potential WRNS supply officers now attend the Junior Supply Officers' Course to acquire these skills.

Another specialisation closely aligned with the male Service is communications, and work in headquarters and operational establishments will occupy not only a high proportion of communications specialists but WRNS operations officers, who may include those specially trained in automatic data processing and Fleet analysis. They may also in future see more of another group of specialisations, concerning intelligence work and photographic interpretation; up to now these have tended to be further back in the intelligence chain.

The air side of the Service sees a good deal of WRNS officers not only secretarial, staff and Fleet analysis, but instructor meteorological and air traffic control specialisations are represented at air stations, and the first WRNS air engineer officer is under training.

Finally, a number of WRNS officers have specialised in careers and personnel selection work, and this small branch is expected to continue, as is the limited number employed in public relations.

Below: A day at sea in HMS *Amazon* **for WRNS officers and ratings from HMS** *Dauntless. Crown Copyright*

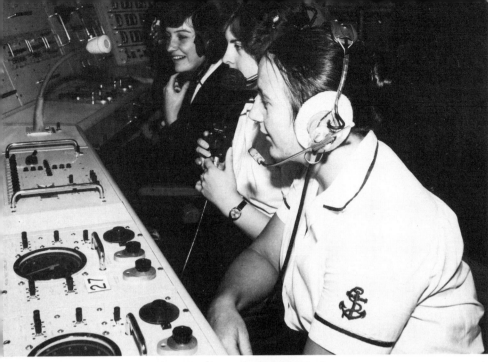

Left: Wrens Radar in the computerised training complex at HMS *Dryad*, **the School of Maritime Operations.** *Crown Copyright*

Below: Wren Radio Operators transmitting taped signal messages. *Crown Copyright*

Rating Structure

WRNS ratings are drawn from the 17-28 age group. There is a test to reflect the academic level of the candidate which all must pass; the pass mark varies from A level standard downwards according to the branch. As well as this there are the usual fitness and nationality requirements, and the number and quality of volunteers is such that high standards can be applied. On joining for new entry training at HMS *Dauntless*, an establishment near Reading which will move to HMS *Raleigh* at Plymouth in mid-1981, a rating has 14 days' probation at the end of which she may leave if she, or the Service, consider that service life is not for her. If she decides to enrol it will be on a nine-year notice engagement with options of further, pensionable service. The commitment of WRNS ratings is thus now very similar to that of their male counterparts. A WRNS rating can, however, leave in order to marry at four months notice at home and six months notice abroad; normal notice is 18 months.

Increasingly, too, training in WRNS categories is aligned with that of the men. But this is not universal; in fact there are 10 WRNS categories which have no male counterpart at all. In the brief account which follows, the branches with male equivalents will be covered first.

In the supply and secretarial field, WRNS ratings are trained for their various specialisations at HMS *Pembroke*, Chatham, Kent. There are three kinds of writer: pay, involving accounting and provision of data for the central computer-operated pay system; general, including secretarial duties, typing and maintaining service records; and shorthand (an exclusive-to-WRNS specialisation) involving more specialised secretarial duties and court-martial work. There are stores accountants who are responsible for custody and issue of all manner of stores from (as the literature has it) sides of beef to sailors' caps. There are stewards who work in officers' messes, waiting at table and serving behind the bar; and finally, cooks who may work in either ships' companies' or officers' galleys. All these important tasks tend to be in categories of chronic or recurring shortage in the male side of the Navy, and the WRNS contribution, to numbers as well as to levels of skill, is an essential one.

The WRNS operations branch falls into two main categories: radar ratings, who are occupied mainly in shore simulators with a large automatic data processing element; and radio operators, who are trained on the modern, highly automated equipments

Above: A Wren cook topping out the trifles at HMS *Daedalus*, Lee-on-Solent. (Photo by Phot Wren Sterck.) *Crown Copyright*

Right: Wren air engineering mechanics. *Crown Copyright*

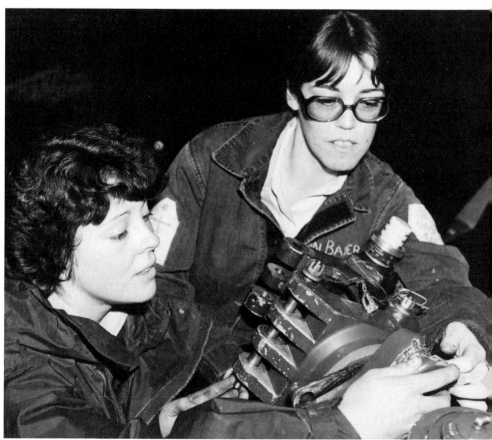

now in service to a level which makes them interchangeable with RN ratings in shore billets.

The same considerations increasingly apply to the popular branches of meteorological observer, photographer and physical training instructor, all of whose duties are fairly self-evident from their titles. The regulating branch, with its responsibility for discipline, drafting and good order, also runs very closely with its male equivalent: ratings for this branch are drawn from other specialisations on attaining a certain seniority.

The engineering branch of the WRNS is at present concerned entirely with aircraft. Air engineering mechanics – who have to meet stiffer educational qualifications than most entrants – can sub-specialise in mechanical, radio or weapons matters and will be employed at air stations, generally on helicopters but with increasing application to all fields. There are outlets to higher grades of technical skill in the mechanician training scheme.

Categories currently exclusive to the WRNS are more fragmented. They include education assistants, who administer education centres and libraries and teach Naval Mathematics and English Test subjects to RN Ratings in the larger establishments; training support assistants, who prepare the numerous aids, both audio and visual, that are used in training establishments; telephonists, dental surgery assistants and hygienists, and motor transport drivers. Weapons analysts assess the results of fleet weapon practices of all kinds, a skilled task and one vital to operational readiness. Some WRNS ratings are specialised in family service work, others in the supervision and administration of WRNS quarters.

Training courses for WRNS categories are mostly held at establishments in the Portsmouth area and last between six and 20 weeks according to the category. In general, Wrens then tend to serve in the naval complexes round Portsmouth, Devonport,

Chatham, Rosyth and the Clyde, and at the Royal Naval Air Stations. There are opportunities further afield, since WRNS billets exist in 12 separate countries, but only in Gibraltar, Brussels and Naples do the complements go into double figures so the chances are limited.

In an establishment, WRNS junior ratings' quarters are separate, generally modern and always well furnished. The part the WRNS can play in the working life of an establishment has already been indicated, but their role in the wider aspects of establishment life is worth dwelling on for a moment. In social activities – based on the ratings' clubs and the officers' messes – and in all forms of recreation from the annual Drama Festival to sailing and gliding events, they are invariably cheerful and active participants. It would be hard to find anyone in the Navy who does not regard them as an enriching and civilising influence, particularly in the remoter establishments.

Promotion ladders for both officers and ratings are very similar to those in the male services. Advancement is within categories, and since some of these are numerically small it is not always quick; on the other hand, the average length of service for WRNS ratings is less than that for men and this tends to keep advancement rosters clear. There are professional qualifying examinations which have to be passed for advancement to both leading and petty officer rate.

Left: A Wren weapons analyst at work in HMS
Daedalus. *Crown Copyright*

Below: A WRNS riding team at Olympia.
Crown Copyright

Right: Expansion of the scope of WRNS activities
will continue: the saluting guns' crew at HMS
Osprey, **Portland**. *Crown Copyright*

Below right: Looking to the future: the first WRNS
air mechanics' course. *Crown Copyright*

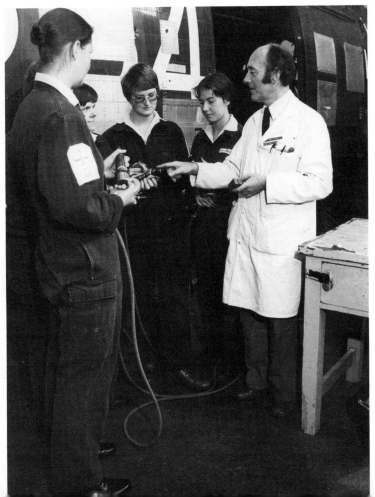

Marriage does not necessarily mean the end of a career in the WRNS. Many girls do leave the Service on marriage – this is, of course, the main reason for the shorter average length of women's service – but others, who are prepared to serve wherever they are needed, continue to do so. They are as entitled to married quarters as male ratings; and in the cases, not infrequent, where a WRNS officer or rating marries a male member of the Service, every effort is made to draft them to the same establishment or area.

The Future

The next ten years are likely to be an important time for the WRNS. The demographic trough of the middle and late 1980s, when the number of young males available for recruitment in a still all-volunteer Service will have shrunk to an extent where the Services' share of the total pool needs to approach 12%, means that women are bound to be more relied on.

Consequently it is likely that the scope of WRNS tasks will expand. The Equal Opportunities Act is not the principal reason for this; though it may be taken as a legal symbol of a sensible and unprejudiced progress towards full participation in naval tasks, it will not be comprehensively implemented in the Service since no plans exist for giving women combat duties.

Short of that, though, there are plenty of extra areas where their participation is likely to be welcome. First, in general terms, they will become more integrated with the male side of the Service. Already officers of the WRNS are doing officer-of-the-day duties in establishments; and since the OOD is the captain's direct representative, that is a quite far-reaching step. There will be increasing integration into the command and divisional structure at all levels; male ratings will no longer be surprised if a WRNS officer is in charge of their division. How long it will take for the blue stripes and badges of the WRNS to be replaced by gold – a final and, one suspects, emotive piece of symbolic logic – is a matter for conjecture.

In the specialisations, there will clearly be a move towards further alignment of both officers and ratings with their male counterparts. It may be necessary to stretch imagination a bit in certain categories – for instance, it will not be easy to equate seaman lieutenant-commanders who have done the Advanced Warfare Course and ship command examination with a WRNS First Officer of the intelligence or fleet analysis specialisation, but there is not likely to be a closer equivalent. Moreover, some careful vertical co-ordination between WRNS officer and rating categories will be needed; in some places, notably supply and secretariat, the 'fit' is already pretty good, but in others – say air traffic control and dentistry – it scarcely exists.

That said, expansion can be foreseen in the officers' specialisations of air engineering, intelligence, air traffic control, communications, operations and instructor; while automatic data processing qualifications will increasingly be a prerequisite for a variety of tasks. Ratings' specialisations likely to increase are air engineering mechanics and mechanicians, weapons electrical mechanics (a new category), writers, drivers and stores

accountants. There will be some trail-blazing to do, for the most enterprising, in aircrew duties – initially in non-combatant helicopters, later perhaps in ferry work – in hydrography, and in air engineering.

Finally, there are the two most emotive questions of all; will women fight, and will they go to sea? The first question has already been answered in the negative, though the more operational women's tasks become, the more likely they are to get involved in combat willy-nilly. As for going to sea, fleet analysts already do this generally on a day-running basis, and air engineering mechanics are likely to go with their helicopter flights to RFAs. The trend is there and will continue: generally women will be visitors and join ships on a temporary attachment, but certainly the writer does not see this to be a hard-and-fast rule. For example, there is much to be said for giving opportunities to women in the surveying service, though this would entail their being part of the permanent ships' companies.

There is no doubt that the WRNS, under a succession of far-sighted and most able directors, and with wholehearted support from the male side of the Service, have set themselves a worthwhile, rewarding and immensely helpful programme of development for the 1980s and beyond.

Postscript: In order not to give a misleadingly buoyant impression, it must be said that the latest information (October 1981) suggests that overall numbers in the WRNS will fall over the next decade, and that some of the added scope of duties may not be easy to achieve. This does not invalidate the essential conclusion that the WRNS still has a most valuable part to play.

Right: A leading Wren photographer attached to the search and rescue flight at HMS
Daedalus. Crown Copyright

10

Organisation and Training

When, some years ago, a group of Senior Officers were discussing a major reorganisation of the Royal Navy's command structure, they became involved in problems of definition. What, exactly, did 'organisation' mean? Worse, what did 'administration' mean? They concluded that administration was what organisation did most of the time, and organisation was something that did administration.

The writer cannot do better, but can try to put it another way. To use the dangerous analogy of the human body, organisation can be likened to the brain and central nervous system, administration to the direction of that system for the maintenance of the body in good condition; to extend the analogy a trifle, training is the familiarisation of every member of the body in the functions it is expected to conduct, and operational command and control is the direction, through the nervous system, of the conduct of those functions.

The analogy is not, of course, a precise one, and this is nowhere more apparent than in the higher reaches of Naval organisation, where not only are there many tiers of decision-making but the decisions concerned are of very different kinds. For example, as civil servants are fond of saying, the Ministry of Defence is a department of State and not a headquarters, and this makes it qualitatively different from the office of a commander-in-chief as well as occupying a superior place in the hierarchy.

The Ministry of Defence
Within the Ministry of Defence, under the Secretary of State and in co-ordination with the Central Staffs, the Navy Department makes policy and the plans to implement it, and carries out the necessary dealings with outside agencies. Major policy decisions are taken by the Admiralty Board, which is presided over by a Minister and includes the First Sea Lord, who is the professional head of the Service, the other three Sea Lords and the Vice Chief of Naval Staff, as well as senior civil servants. Advice to the Board – and of course decision-making at a lower level – is provided by the Naval Staff on policy matters, which include the size and shape of the Fleet and the strategy for its employment, and by the rest of the Navy Department on personnel, material and support matters. Civilian participation in the process of advice and decision-making is universal.

The high technical and material content of naval forces, and the fact that so much of design and development is in service or official hands, entails participation by Naval and, more markedly, civilian personnel in the Procurement Executive both at London and Bath and at research and development establishments. Nor does the delegation of development work to a firm absolve the Navy Department from responsibility, since constant monitoring and proving of the result is necessary.

Thus, a great deal of the policy and provision of the Navy comes down from the Ministry of Defence. But detailed management comes under the two commanders-in-chief: C-in-C Fleet, with his headquarters at Northwood, and C-in-C Naval Home Command, at Portsmouth.

C-in-C Fleet
The Commander-in-Chief, Fleet, has under command all the operational ships and submarines, and embarked aircraft, of the Royal Navy. His headquarters near London is convenient for the essential operational co-ordination with the Royal Air Force – the commander of the long-range maritime reconnaisance element is co-located at Northwood and the AOC-in-C Strike Command close by at High Wycombe – and for communication with the Ministry of Defence, and not inconvenient for visiting the ships of the Fleet, which he frequently does. The Flag Officer, Submarines, is also at Northwood.

Surface ships are divided into three flotillas, each under the command of a flag officer. These are the officers who, in general, can be expected to take charge at sea of group deployments, of task groups in NATO or national exercises, and of course in operations if required. Under them there is further subdivision into squadrons under a captain, so that for example all Ikara Leanders at present are commanded by the Captain, 1st Frigate Squadron. All these senior officers are supported by appropriate staffs so that material and personnel can be satisfactorily administered.

C-inC Naval Home Command
The Commander-in-Chief, Naval Home Command, has under command all naval shore establishments, except naval air stations, in the United Kingdom and has overall responsibility for co-ordinating the implementation of training policy as laid down by the Admiralty Board. These responsibilities give him about the same number of servicemen under command as the C-in-C Fleet. The main concentration of training establishments round Portsmouth is a powerful factor in the location of his headquarters. But, of course, there are other concentrations, particularly in the Plymouth, Chatham and Rosyth areas, and in those areas as well as at Portsmouth the Commander-in-Chief has flag officers to take some of the administrative load off his shoulders though he still takes direct responsibility for training standards.

Port administration for support of the Fleet is the responsibility of Port admirals, who at Devonport, Portsmouth and Chatham are the flag officers themselves. At Rosyth they are separate individuals. Again, staffs at these bases deal with all the matters of detail – communication, recording, co-ordination, direction – that go to make up that complex process called administration.

NATO Aspects
Nearly every commander so far mentioned has a corresponding NATO function which he carries out in exercises, tension or war and for which he may sometimes have a permanent multi-national staff. Thus, C-in-C Fleet is also the Commander, Eastern Atlantic Area (CINCEASTLANT) and Allied Commander-in-Chief Channel; Flag Officer Plymouth is also Commander, Central Atlantic Area under CINCEASTLANT and the Commander of the Plymouth sub-area of the Channel Command.

Training
But if the end-product is to be a Navy that is ready, from admiral to ordinary seaman, to carry out NATO and other operational

Right: Her Majesty the Queen, Lord High Admiral of the United Kingdom, presents a telescope to the senior Sub-Lieutenant at a passing-out parade at the Britannia Royal Naval College, Dartmouth. (Photo by Mr C. Risk). *Crown Copyright*

Below: The Admiralty Board, 5 February 1981. From left: Mr A. A. Pritchard, Deputy Under-Secretary (Navy); Mr Keith Speed, MP, Under-Secretary of State for Defence for the Royal Navy; Sir Arthur Hockaday, Second Permanent Under-Secretary, Ministry of Defence; Mr A. Cragg, Head of Defence Secretariat, Division 4; Admiral Sir Henry Leach, First Sea Lord; Sir John Charnley, Controller, R and D Establishments and Research; Admiral Sir Desmond Cassidi, Second Sea Lord; Admiral Sir John Fieldhouse, Controller of the Navy; Vice-Admiral Sir William Pillar, Chief of Fleet Support; Vice-Admiral William Staveley, Vice Chief of Naval Staff. *Crown Copyright*

tasks and thereby deter aggression, the path to that readiness must lie in a carefully thought out and thoroughly implemented training programme both ashore and afloat. The rest of this chapter covers, all too briefly, some aspects of the training pattern.

Officers

In any ship's wardroom, enquiry will quickly show that the officers have reached their current rank by several different routes. This one may have decided to join the Royal Navy while at university; another may have had no other ambition since he was ten, got a reserved place after interview by the Admiralty Interview Board at the age of 16, and gone to Dartmouth after passing his 'A' levels; another may have joined as a rating with good educational qualifications, have been selected early as an officer and now be in the main career stream; a fourth may have become a petty officer at 25 and then decided to acquire the necessary qualifications and recommendation for the Special Duties List.

The ways are diverse and even bewildering, and the right place for a detailed description is the recruiting literature and not this book. But some common elements are worth identifying here. First, all aspiring officers, except doctors and dentists, have to pass the Admiralty Interview Board, which uses its fund of experience to judge whether a candidate's character, abilities and potential measure up to the Service. Second, all career officers will do some time at the Britannia Royal Naval College, Dartmouth, and some time under training in the Fleet, to become

Above: Boats from the Royal Naval College racing off Dartmouth. (Photo by Mr C. Risk). *Crown Copyright*

Left: One way of crossing the Dart: cadets under training. (Photo by Mr C. Risk). *Crown Copyright*

Above: More conventional sports are also catered for at the Britannia Royal Naval College. (Photo by Mr C. Risk). *Crown Copyright*

Right: Sea training for Midshipmen in HMS *Intrepid's* **machinery control room.** *Crown Copyright*

accustomed to the ways of the sea and of the Navy, to acquire and practise basic skills and leadership, and to have their suitability for a Service career confirmed. Finally, all will specialise either as seamen, engineer, supply and secretariat or instructor officers and, after their Fleet training, do further courses to qualify them in these specialisations. Such training does not necessarily finish here. For example, between the ages of 24 and 26 a seaman might expect to do a lieutenant's course followed by a Principal Warfare Officer's Course to enable him to take charge of an operations room in the prime state at sea, and at 33 an Advanced Warfare Course; but if he sub-specialised in, say, flying or hydrography, the pattern would be different. An engineer would go to the Royal Naval Engineering College for degree and application courses which lead to fully chartered status. Supply and secretariat officers have another typical pattern, with a blend of sea and shore time and a further hurdle in the Supply Charge Course before appointment as supply officer of a ship. Instructor officers generally enter as graduates and the bulk are employed ashore teaching, often to very advanced standards; but they can expect some sea time, particularly in the meteorological sub-specialisation. Subsequent academic challenges for all officers could be the Staff Course at Greenwich, or the National Defence College at Latimer, in their early and mid-thirties.

Short service careers, some of as little as three and a half years' duration, are increasingly popular, requiring as they do less initial commitment and rather lower educational qualifications than a full career. In these forms of commission specialisation can be narrower, and this particularly applies to flying (the minimum length of service here is eight years), where passage through Dartmouth is relatively brisk, there is no Fleet time and after successful completion of his flying training a pilot or observer can be expected to be employed as such throughout his time in the Navy unless, of course, he is accepted for transfer to a full career commission, in which case he will wish, and be expected, to broaden his experience.

Ratings

The alternative methods of entry for ratings are scarcely less varied than those for officers, and their subsequent paths are even more diverse. The most usual way of joining is as a junior from 16 to 17½ years of age, though adult entries from 17½ to 33 are equally acceptable. Recruiting tests, mental and physical, are simple but not slack; the Navy has learnt to its cost that setting too low a standard results only in high drop-out rates and much disappointment and waste.

Initial training for entrants is at HMS *Raleigh* in the West Country, where a short sharp five-week course accustoms the young sailor to service discipline and standards as well as teaching basic skills. Those who wish to stay on in the Navy – there is an option of leaving in the first few months – go on to specialist training, mostly at other establishments, in the operations, engineering, supply and secretariat or air branches. The number of sub-specialisations runs into dozens: examples are radar, mine warfare, radio operator (tactical), cook, weapon engineering mechanic, stores accountant; courses for both specialisations and sub-specialisations may amount to 20-30 weeks. After that a rating goes, as soon as may be, to sea, and thereafter may advance through the ratings of leading hand, petty officer and chief petty officer to the ultimate and very responsible rate of fleet chief petty officer, a full equivalent of warrant rank in the other Services. All these steps require the acquisition of further qualifications, experience and recommendations. Sea and shore service tend to alternate, with periods in a ship usually two years or less.

There is still a need at sea for the advanced technical skills that only an apprenticeship can provide. The artificer rate is essential, therefore, and there are at present nine specialisations in maintenance and repair skills which give a man petty officer rate soon after completing his five-year apprenticeship and quick advancement to chief petty officer rate thereafter. Educational qualifications are, of course, more stringent for this entry than for the general run of ratings. Artificer levels of skill can also be

Left: **Rating entries at HMS** *Raleigh* **are introduced to a dry seaboat . . .**

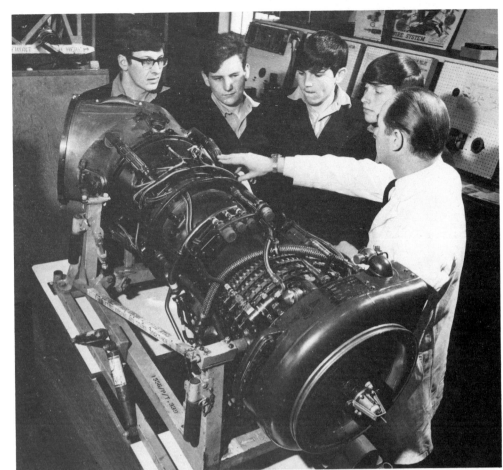

Left: . . . and anchors and cables. *Crown Copyright*

Below left: One of many rating specialisations: stewards under training, supervised by a petty officer steward. *Crown Copyright*

Right: Instruction on the Gnome engine fuel computer system at the RN Air Electrical School, HMS *Daedalus*, Lee-on-Solent. *Crown Copyright*

Below: An artificer apprentice under training at HMS *Fisgard*. *Crown Copyright*

Above: **Under training at Dartmouth for the Special Duties List. Over 25% of Naval Officers began their careers on the lower deck. (Photo by Mr C. Risk).** *Crown Copyright*

attained by mechanic branch ratings after training as mechanicians.

As has already been mentioned, ratings may become officers on getting the necessary qualifications: either early on, at 19 or so, to join the main career stream, or later, and with lower educational requirements, to join the Special Duties List which has promotion prospects as far as commander. Well over 25% of all officers in the Royal Navy began their careers on the lower deck.

The Medical Services

Doctors and dentists enter the Royal Navy after qualifying as such, though some may have obtained cadetships while still students and thereby have been helped financially – with a commitment to a five-year short career commission on qualifying. While the Royal Navy operates two hospitals at Haslar, near Portsmouth, and Stonehouse, Plymouth, a smaller hospital at Gibraltar and sick quarters at other bases, medical and dental

officers can expect to spend a proportion of their time afloat. For example, each Polaris submarine crew includes a doctor and all large ships have dental as well as medical staffs.

Medical ratings fall into two categories: Assistants, who have a general training enabling them to become the only medically trained person in many small ships, with the opportunity of further specialisation; and technicians, who may include those with State Registered Nurse (SRN) qualifications and work in the highly skilled and therapeutic fields of modern medicines such as radiography and physiotherapy.

Finally, Queen Alexandra's Royal Naval Nursing Service (QARNNS), now open to both men and women, completes the naval medical services. They do not serve at sea, but are represented in 26 shore establishments including, of course, the two main naval hospitals. Nursing officers must have the State Registered Nurse qualification. Length of engagement and commitment is now in line with that of the WRNS.

Chaplains

In the Royal Navy a chaplain has no rank other than chaplain and that of his office in the church, with all the approachability that that status brings. Any one who has served in the Royal Navy will know the influence on the life of a naval community that can be exerted by a chaplain; this has not slackened in modern times. Chaplains of all denominations serve ashore and afloat, and with Royal Marines Commando forces. Men who have been ordained for three years or more enter initially on a four-year short service commission with the opportunity to extend to a full career.

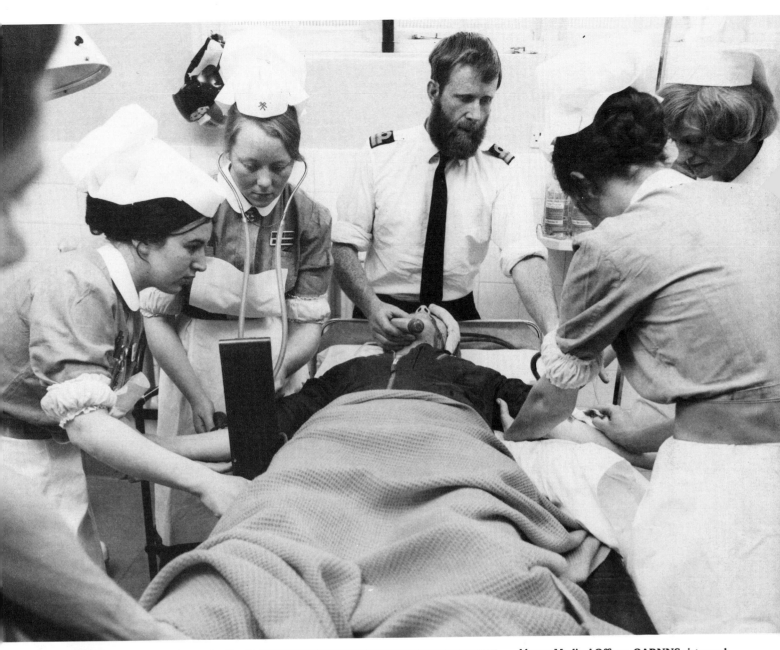

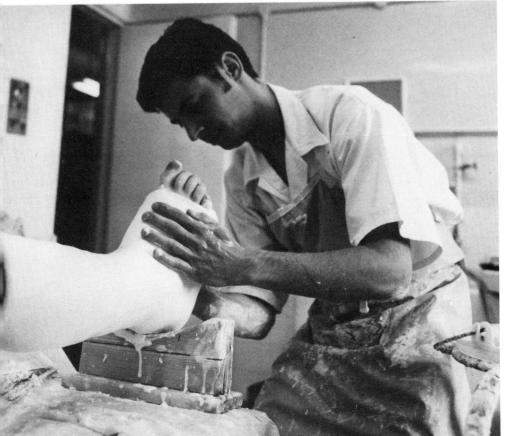

Above: Medical Officer, QARNNS sister and nurses. *Crown Copyright*

Left: A medical technician applies a plaster cast. *Crown Copyright*

127

Above: On the sweep deck of HMS *Upton*, **a Royal Naval Reserve Minesweeper.** *Crown Copyright*

Right: A Royal Naval Auxiliary Service vessel and its Commander, Mrs Denise St. Aubyn Hubbard. *Crown Copyright*

Below right: Simulators ashore save valuable training time particularly in teaching basic procedures. A control panel at the School of Maritime Operations, HMS *Dryad*. *Crown Copyright*

The Reserves

The Royal Fleet Reserve consists of men and women who have recently left the regular Service and can therefore be considered fully trained as well as, by their terms of service, available to be recalled in emergency. The Royal Naval Reserve, some 5,000 strong at present, consists of volunteers who give up one evening or more a week, and a fortnight each year, to be trained in operational tasks such as mine countermeasures, offshore operations, naval control of shipping and manning shore headquarters. It includes, in List 1, many Merchant Navy officers who bring to it their own particular professionalism and expertise. Finally, the 2,400 members of the Royal Naval Auxiliary Service are trained to provide local support in the area of their homes to the naval effort in time of need; typically, they would help to man port heaquarters and run naval port organisations. While no doubt in any protracted conflict these various organisations would be but a nucleus for expansion, their existence and training in peacetime is a vital contribution to maritime readiness.

The Sharp End of Training

Training in the Royal Navy is directed to the achievement of specific objectives: that is, given levels of knowledge and skill both theoretical and related to the systems most commonly encountered in service. This applies to career and advancement courses. Even so, when a man is about to join a ship or squadron, particularly if it is of a class unfamiliar to him, he needs deeper training in those particular systems of that class with which he will have to deal. Pre-joining training to help achieve this is run at all the main schools: for example, marine engineering at HMS *Sultan*, weapons and electrical engineering at HMS *Collingwood*, maritime operations at HMS *Dryad*, air engineering at HMS *Daedalus*. Simulators are extensively used, for though they cannot entirely reproduce the conditions and problems to be met at sea they go far enough to give excellent instruction and practice in all procedures, both team and individual, that go to make up the effective maintenance and operation of modern sea systems. As an example, the School of Maritime Operations, HMS *Dryad*, provides operations rooms modelled precisely on certain classes of ship and operating, so far as digital ingenuity can devise, in the same way, and here ships' teams can work up their procedures and skills in the business of collecting information, assessing tactical situations and controlling forces and weapons to deal with them.

But the sea waits at the end of the road, and is a tougher environment than the most complex simulator. It is the Royal Navy's policy, therefore, to put all ships through the sea training organisation at Portland. Ships no longer recommission fully; replacements 'trickle' through; consequently the various forms of sea training a ship can do, and when she does them, tend to be related more to her refit cycle than to personnel factors. The organisation is in the charge of the Flag Officer, Sea Training, whose staff ensure that every aspect of a ship's likely activity, from missile firing to ceremonial entry into harbour, is practised and tested. A direct descendant from Admiral Stevenson's famous organisation at Tobermory in World War II, the Portland complex aims to ensure that ships are ready for anything, and its success can be judged not only from the eagerness with which NATO allies send their ships for work up, but from the resilience and resource which has been apparent in the Royal Navy's work over recent years.

Below: Frigates leaving Portland for operational sea training.
Crown Copyright

The Future

So far as organisation goes, it seems unlikely that the present arrangements will change much in the next few years. The major reorganisation under two Commanders-in-Chief, which occurred just over ten years ago, was logical and appears irreducible. Adjustments and rationalisations will occur but upheavals will be avoided.

Entry, engagement and training are more volatile matters. Entry will have to take into account of factors both outside and within the Navy. The main external factors will be the demographic trough encountered in the late 1980s, and the enployment situation in the country at large. The critical internal factors will be the size and shape of the Fleet that has to be manned, and the number of shore billets that absolutely need to be filled in order to keep that Fleet at sea in a trained and efficient state. Engagements will tend to be on an ever more open basis but with reward for extra commitment; further allowance is likely to be made for those who want to make the Royal Navy fill their working lifetimes; so, effectively, there will be even more flexibility of engagement from very short to very long. Finally, training will have to take account of ever more complex technical and operational problems, though these may be offset by increasing reliance on repair by replacement and computer-aided operating techniques.

All these factors interact, and in doing so they present formidable challenges. One is driven to the conclusion that everyone in the Navy will have to be brave as a lion, cunning as a fox, and tough as old boots; that no society can be expected to offer these qualities ready-made in abundance; and that moreover there will be many occupations in the naval service which in civilian life would carry 'officer' status but in the RN canot do so. There will, therefore, be problems in incentive, in catchment and in training.

Yet I would confidently predict that the Navy will go on succeeding in this most difficult, and fundamentally important, of all its tasks. The moment a well-motivated boy or girl joins, is subject to healthy and properly-directed discipline, and has his or her mind stretched in a way that starts to exploit its potential, all the latent qualities begin to be seen, and self-confidence and self-respect grow. Anyone who has served in a training establishment has seen this over and over again. It gives one renewed faith in the human spirit, and in the underlying spirit of the Nation.

Below: Sea training: arming a Wasp helicopter with torpedoes on board HMS *Ambuscade. Crown Copyright*

11

A Pattern of Operations

Few things are so liable to error as the prediction of the course of future conflict, particularly after a long period without major warfare but with profound technological change. Therefore, in this final chapter which aims to draw together the characteristics of the Royal Navy as they have previously been described and show how they might be employed in action, I shall have to admit to speculation; and by firmly using the first person singular, I hope to imply that this is one individual's view of a matter on which there may be many opinions.

The situation to be discussed is what we may call the 'determinant case': the beginning of a major conflict on land and sea between the Warsaw Pact and NATO, in which the maritime forces of the United Kingdom have to bear the brunt in the Eastern Atlantic of a determined Soviet effort to cut the Atlantic reinforcement route and in the North Sea and Channel of an attempt to block ports and approaches, and where additionally the United Kingdom is called on to help Norway resist a Soviet land assault in the North.

Several caveats must be entered at once. First, I am not saying this is the only likely situation for major conflict; on the contrary, it is a rather unlikely situation because of the deterrent paradox which says that the better you are at fighting a certain sort of war, the less likely is your opponent to embark on that sort of war. The point is that a general conflict of this nature is a particularly damaging sort of war for the West, and therefore one that it particularly wants to deter; in consequence preparations for such a conflict must be an important factor in the choice of force structures. Second, I am not saying that this sort of conflict is all that the Royal Navy is for. On the contrary, I have argued that the Navy's work and deterrent effect extend through peacetime conditions and low intensity operations, and may stretch far beyond the NATO area; and that account should be taken of this in its organisation and deployment, and in the characteristics of its material and training. But that does not absolve it from the need to compete successfully in the 'determinant case'.

Western Objectives
The main lines of Soviet maritime effort have been described above. Western objectives would include the passing of supplies running into several millions of tons from the United States to the European theatre; deployment of many hundreds of thousands of men from the USA and United Kingdom to Europe; checking any Soviet advance in Norway; holding the Baltic straits; and ensuring that strategic deterrent forces at sea remain secure. On these premises it is unrealistic to the point of absurdity to suggest that the supply or reinforcement tasks can be met by air transport alone; as absurd, perhaps, as to suggest that a conflict will last so short a time as to make reinforcement irrelevant. Anyone holding the latter view is either planning to lose, or planning to initiate the very early use of nuclear weapons; the one is unattractive, the other requires only tripwire forces in Europe, and neither is close to NATO's flexible-response strategy.

Soviet Forces
Taking figures from unclassified publications and allowing two-thirds operational availability, one can calculate that the Soviet Northern Fleet could deploy some 30 strategic and 90 tactical submarines; a quarter of the latter could be cruise missile-armed and rather under half nuclear-powered. Major surface combatants deployed could amount to 55 or so, and aircraft armed with air-to-surface missiles about 70. If the Baltic Fleet were able to break out, these numbers would be augmented considerably; and in any event it would be prudent to allow for the Baltic Fleet Air Force, with perhaps 50 missile-armed aircraft, to penetrate beyond the Danish straits.

The ranges of Soviet tactical missiles are of much relevance. Generally speaking, submarine-to-surface missiles have effective ranges of tens of miles; surface-to-surface missiles one or two hundred miles; and air-to-surface missiles from 150 to 450 miles. All missiles are probably able to carry nuclear warheads. A very recent development in the form of a submerged-launch missile with a range of some hundreds of miles sharpens, but does not fundamentally alter, the problem.

Finally, some indication of tactical doctrine can be found in the writings of Gorshkov. It is certain that he has taken two of Jacky Fisher's dicta to heart: 'Hit first, hit hard'. Soviet forces can be expected to try to take up marking positions within missile range of Western units before hostilities open and great emphasis would be put on getting in co-ordinated attacks as soon after their onset as possible. Whether the third part of Fisher's admonition, 'Keep on hitting', is so much part of Soviet doctrine is debatable; but their units are well-defended and lack of durability should not be assumed.

Western Dispositions
There are some things the West would very much want to do before hostilities opened: to establish Royal Marine Commandos in Northern Norway, to call up reservists, to set up Naval Control of Shipping and port defence organisations. Such moves would require swift political decision after an assessment that hostilities were likely; they would also require well-exercised means for their implementation, and these at present exist in *Hermes* and her helicopter squadrons, and in the volunteer forces of the RNR and RNXS. If successful such measures might, indeed, deter further deterioration of the situation.

However, if that desirable outcome did not happen, the initial dispositions of Western maritime forces would be of the utmost importance. Given Soviet doctrine, no commander would wish to set up all his ducks in a row to be shot at at Soviet initiative. On the other hand, some at least must be close enough to operational areas to ensure a brisk start to the job of keeping reinforcement routes open. An ugly game of hide and seek, watched over by satellites and listened to by all available intelligence gathering devices, can be predicted. In this game, a great reassurance to British surface units will be their high level of training and ability to sustain prime state manning for indefinite periods, their sophisticated area and point air defence systems and their good sensor, communications, command and control arrangements.

Help from allies could, of course, be expected. The Dutch intend to provide two task groups in the Atlantic; the French have always said they will support the Alliance on the day. The German and Danish navies are committed to the defence of the

Naval forces have many peacetime tasks but these do not absolve them of the need to be effective in war

Left: **Winning friends and influencing people, Mombasa.** *Crown Copyright*

Right: **HMS** *Antrim* **berths at Shanghai.** *Crown Copyright*

Below: **On patrol in the Gulf of Oman, 1981: HM Ships** *Birmingham* **and** *Avenger*, **RFAs** *Fort Austin* **and** *Olmeda*. **Three Sea King and two Lynx helicopters are airborne astern of the ships.** *Crown Copyright*

Baltic straits and are unlikely to have much left over for the Atlantic. Finally, and most powerfully, the United States Strike Fleet, when deployed, would be a critical factor in any battle; but initially, at any rate, it may well be elsewhere. There would however be great help from information systems based in the continental United States, from their fleet submarines, and from maritime aircraft operating from Iceland.

A Pattern of Operations

The initial task of the Royal Navy, then, will be to survive the 'first salvo' on which Gorshkov puts so much emphasis; and it will need a mixture of strength and cunning. Not for the last time, the ability to complicate the opponent's problems will be an important factor: Sea Harriers with their ability to disrupt shadowing activity which is so critical to co-ordinated longrange missile attack; ceaseless patrols by anti-submarine helicopters; the co-operation of the Royal Air Force in surveillance; countermarking by our own submarines of marking units; above all the ability to control the manoeuvres of diverse forces in a way that maximises the enemy's confusion but keeps our own disorder at a minimum. Of course the first salvo, unless it is unexpectedly ineffective or pre-empted, will sink some units; of course others will be damaged. For the latter, sturdy construction, duplicated systems and good training may make the difference between life and death.

The main task of the surviving forces will be to safeguard the reinforcement routes. Here I must express a personal view that convoy, or something like it, would be a feature of reinforcement operations. Without such a focus for defence, nuclear and conventionally-powered enemy submarines would be able to pick off shipping more or less at will, and however great a menace certain contingencies, such as enemy nuclear submarines keeping station under a convoy, might be, the risks overall must be less. This said, many kinds of variation on the large, symmetrical convoy with a close escort are possible.

This is because not only have submarine speeds and weapon ranges much increased, but so have anti-submarine sensor and weapon ranges. 'Area Defence' is therefore a reasonable concept in the underwater sphere, and one can envisage areas hundreds of miles across where no submarine being used tactically can regard itself as immune from detection and destruction. The focus for such areas would, naturally, be a surface combatant group, probably in support rather than escort of a convoy or convoys, consisting ideally of an *Invincible* class ship with its embarked helicopters and VSTOL aircraft, several type 22 and 42 ships, and backed in the deep field by long range patrol aircraft and fleet submarines. Co-ordination of these forces, and information exchange between them, would be crucial; but with satellite communications and the equipment in the bigger surface ships, this is well catered for.

A particularly important area for such support groups is the mid-Atlantic ridge. Here, in relatively shallow water, sonic ocean surveillance systems are less effective than elsewhere, and the distance from RAF bases is so long that the loiter time even of long range maritime patrol aircraft is limited. Moreover this location is far from the Soviet Naval Air Force bases and this would give the maximum chance of blunting the inevitable air attacks. So support groups would pay their maximum dividends here. Logistically they would be supported by an underway replenishment group of Royal Fleet Auxiliaries with embarked helicopters and an escort mainly of frigates.

Consider the progress of a Soviet submarine bent on attacking the reinforcement route from the Northern Fleet area. On its long transit south it must risk detection from ocean surveillance systems, patrolling fleet submarines and aircraft-laid sonobuoy barriers in the Greenland-Iceland-Faeroes-U.K. gaps. Once approaching the convoy routes, it must run the gauntlet of long range maritime air patrols, ships and submarines using passive towed arrays, helicopters deploying sonobuoys. If it survives – and modern anti-submarine torpedoes are designed to ensure a quick kill if it is detected and localised – to get in an attack, then retribution, in the form of helicopter or surface ship detection by active or passive sonar and subsequent attack, is a probability.

Consider also an air attack developed from the northern airfields at Olenya or Severomorsk. This could be in regimental strength, by Badger or Backfire missile-carrying aircraft. NATO radar chains would detect them soon after passing North Cape; they would be subject to attack by landbased aircraft on their way south. Closer to their target they might have to contend with opposition from Sea Harriers; certainly any co-operating shadower would have to do so. Finally, the missiles after release would have to run the gauntlet of Sea Dart and Sea Wolf missiles, and be resistant to the seductions of electronic jammers and chaff decoys, in order to reach their targets.

Finally, consider a Soviet surface unit aiming to deliver a missile attack on a NATO force in mid-Atlantic. It would be threatened by RAF strike aircraft from the United Kingdom, by Sea Harriers from their carrier, by fleet submarines armed with Harpoon missiles and torpedoes throughout its transit, and by surface action groups armed with Exocet – and their Lynxes armed with Sea Skua – on approaching its quarry. After launch, Soviet missiles would still have the same obstacles to pass as air-launched missiles.

None of this is to say that countering attacks from the advanced and highly capable Soviet naval forces is easy, cheap or assured in every case. It is to say rather that defence in depth, in all these fields, is a prerequisite of survival let alone success. That defence in depth is provided by the naval capabilities and programmes described in this book, not as comprehensively as many in the Service would like nor with as much assurance for the future as is

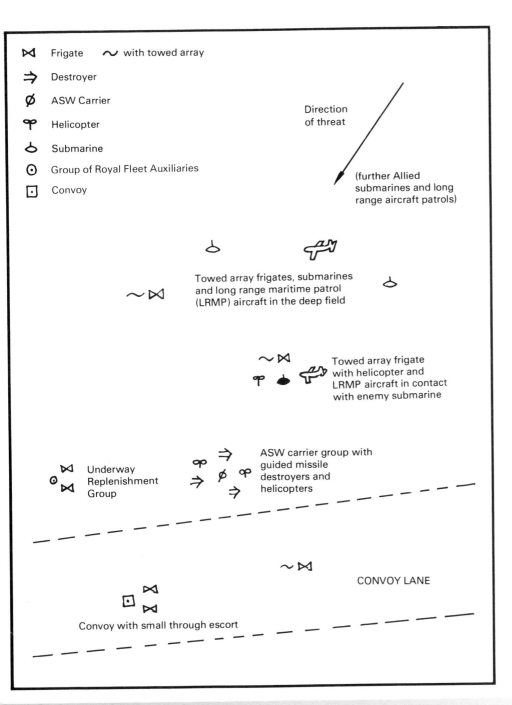

Frigate ∼ with towed array

Destroyer

ASW Carrier

Helicopter

Submarine

Group of Royal Fleet Auxiliaries

Convoy

Direction
of threat

(further Allied
submarines and long
range aircraft patrols)

Towed array frigates, submarines
and long range maritime patrol
(LRMP) aircraft in the deep field

Towed array frigate
with helicopter and
LRMP aircraft in contact
with enemy submarine

ASW carrier group with
guided missile
destroyers and
helicopters

Underway
Replenishment
Group

CONVOY LANE

Convoy with small through escort

Far left: NATO forces at readiness: the Standing Naval Force, Atlantic. But the chief burden in the Eastern Atlantic falls to the Royal Navy. *Crown Copyright*

Left: One way of tackling the determinant case: a possible disposition for United Kingdom support forces in mid-Atlantic. *Author's Copyright*

Below: To keep cross-Channel routes open, vigorous mine counter-measures will be required: Royal Naval Reserve minesweepers at sea. *Crown Copyright*

needed for full confidence, but at least to a much greater degree than in any other navy of Western Europe. When, in such a conflict as I have described, the United States can bring its full force to bear in the Atlantic, its arrival will no doubt be greeted with the same sort of reception as the sheriff's posse in a western film. But for the first vital days, the autonomy of the British maritime forces will be a key factor.

One further aspect of defence in depth must be mentioned, however briefly. This is the ability to fight at the tactical nuclear level. The Soviet Navy's capacity in this field is well known, and however strong one's hunch may be that the Russians would be slow to cross the nuclear threshold at sea, the Royal Navy must clearly be able to ride out, and retaliate in kind against, nuclear attack without recourse to strategic weapons. This it is equipped to do.

Other Theatres

In the approaches to the submarine bases on the Clyde, it will be necessary to conduct minesweeping operations and any other activities necessary to keep and if possible reinforce the strategic deterrent at sea. For such operations the Hunt class mine countermeasures vessels are essential, and so may be nuclear-powered submarines and some surface craft.

For cross-Channel and cross-North Sea operations, the two essentials will be mine countermeasures – particularly mine-hunting – and control of shipping, not only in ports but at sea. The offshore patrol vessels will be invaluable here; suggestions that they have no war role are nonsense; every ship with a white ensign will be needed to improve organisation and control. In such operations, too, the Reserves would play an absolutely essential part both ashore and afloat. Once again, training and dedication in peacetime is a forerunner of operational success.

Envoi

Perhaps that is a good note on which to end. This book has described the third most powerful navy in the world, a key and unique contribution to the Western Alliance, full of technical innovation and high quality equipment. As my preface, written after the Government announcements of June 1981, suggests, I think it will go on being that. It will work to its best effect if its political direction is consistent and well-judged, if its material procurement is imaginative and economical, if its support is well organised and if it can recruit people of the right calibre, train them well and retain their commitment and dedication. Probably that last set of factors is the most important of all. In the long run, it is people that are navies, as they are nations.

Below: What it's all about: the ship and the sea. . .

Right: . . . but the man is the greatest single factor. *Crown Copyright*

Appendices

1 The Ships and Squadrons of the Royal Navy in November 1981

Ships in the Standby Squadron are indicated thus*
For ships building, no date of completion is shown. Ships on the disposal list are not included. Overall dimensions are given in feet with metric equivalents in brackets.

Name and Pendant Number		Class	When completed	Overall dimensions		
				Length	Beam	Complement
Ballistic missile submarines						
Resolution	(S22)	Polaris				Two crews
Renown	(S26)	Ballistic	1967-9	425	33	of
Repulse	(S23)	Missile		(129.5)	(10.1)	147
Revenge	(S27)	Submarines				
Fleet submarines						
Dreadnought	(S101)	Dreadnought	1963	265	32	113
				(80.8)	(9.7)	
Valiant	(S102)	Valiant	1966-7	285	33	116
Warspite	(S103)			(86.8)	(10.1)	
Churchill	(S104)					
Conqueror	(S105)	Churchill	1968-73	285	33	116
Courageous	(S106)			(86.8)	(10.1)	
Swiftsure	(S126)					
Sovereign	(S108)					
Superb	(S109)	Swiftsure	1973-81	272	33	116
Sceptre	(S110)			(82.9)	(10.1)	
Spartan	(S111)					
Splendid	(S112)					
Trafalgar	(S113)	Trafalgar	Not released			
Turbulent	(S114)					
Patrol Submarines						
Oberon	(S09)					
Odin	(S10)					
Orpheus	(S11)					
Olympus	(S12)					
Osiris	(S13)					
Onslaught	(S14)	Oberon	1960-7	295	26	65
Otter	(S15)			(90)	(7.9)	
Oracle	(S16)					
Ocelot	(S17)					
Otus	(S18)					
Opossum	(S19)					
Opportune	(S20)					
Onyx	(S21)					
*Porpoise	(S01)					
Sealion	(S07)	Porpoise	1958-61	295	26	65
Walrus	(S08)			(90)	(7.9)	
ASW Carriers						
Invincible	(R05)		1979			900
Illustrious		Invincible		677	105	plus air
Ark Royal				(206)	(32)	squadrons

Name and Pendant Number		Class	When completed	Overall dimensions		Complement
				Length	Beam	

ASW/Commando Carrier

Name and Pendant Number		Class	When completed	Length	Beam	Complement
Hermes	(R12)	Hermes	1959	754 (229.8)	90 (27.4)	980 plus air squadrons

Assault Ships

Fearless	(L10)	Fearless	1965-6	520 (158)	80 (24.4)	580
Intrepid	(L11)					

Guided Missile Destroyers

Sheffield	(D80)		1974			
Birmingham	(D86)		1976			
Coventry	(D118)		1978			
Newcastle	(D87)		1978			
Cardiff	(D108)		1979	410 (125)	48 (14.6)	280
Glasgow	(D88)		1979			
Exeter	(D89)	Sheffield (Type 42)	1980			
Southampton	(D90)		1981			
Nottingham	(D91)					
Liverpool	(D92)		1981			
Manchester	(D95)					
Gloucester	(D96)			450 (139)	50 (15.2)	280
York						
Edinburgh						
*London	(D16)					
Glamorgan	(D19)					
Fife	(D20)	County	1962-70	520 (158.5)	54 (16.4)	485
Antrim	(D18)					
Norfolk	(D21)					
Bristol	(D23)	Bristol (Type 82)	1972	507 (154.5)	55 (16.7)	407

Frigates

Broadsword	(F88)		1979			
Battleaxe	(F89)		1979			
Brilliant	(F90)	Broadsword (Type 22)	1981	428.4 (131)	48.1 (14.7)	224
Brazen	(F91)					
Boxer	(F92)					
Beaver						
Amazon	(F169)		1974			
Antelope	(F170)		1975			
Ambuscade	(F172)		1975			
Arrow	(F173)	Amazon (Type 21)	1975	384 (117)	41.7 (12.7)	170
Active	(F171)		1977			
Alacrity	(F174)		1977			
Ardent	(F184)		1977			
Avenger	(F185)		1978			
Leander	(F109)					
Dido	(F104)					
Ajax	(F114)					
Galatea	(F18)	Ikara Leander	1963-5	372 (113.4)	41 (12.5)	240
Naiad	(F39)					
Aurora	(F10)					
Euryalus	(F15)					
Arethusa	(F38)					
Cleopatra	(F28)					
Sirius	(F40)					
Phoebe	(F42)					
Minerva	(F45)	Exocet Leander	1963-7	372 (113.4)	41 (12.5)	230
Danae	(F47)					
Argonaut	(F56)					
Penelope	(F127)					
Andromeda	(F57)					
Hermione	(F58)					
Jupiter	(F60)					
Bacchante	(F69)	Broad-beam Leander	1969-72	372 (113.4)	43 (13.1)	260
Charybdis	(F75)					
Scylla	(F71)					

Name and Pendant Number		Class	When completed	Length	Beam	Complement
Achilles	(F12)	Broad-beam Leander	1969-72	372 (113.4)	43 (13.1)	260
Diomede	(F16)					
Apollo	(F70)					
Ariadne	(F72)					
Juno	(F52)	Leander (modified for training)	1967	372 (113.4)	41 (12.5)	240
Rothesay	(F107)	Rothesay (Type 12)	1960-61	370 (112.8)	41 (12.5)	250
Yarmouth	(F101)					
*Rhyl	(F129)					
Plymouth	(F126)					
*Falmouth	(F113)					
Lowestoft	(F103)					
*Brighton	(F106)					
*Berwick	(F115)					
Londonderry	(F108) ·····(Modified for trials)					

Mine Countermeasure Vessels

Name and Pendant Number		Class	When completed	Length	Beam	Complement
Brecon	(M29)	Hunt (Hunter/ Sweeper)	1979 1981 1981	186.4 (57)	32.7 (10)	
Ledbury	(M30)					
Cattistock						
Cottesmore						
Middleton						
Brocklesby						
Dulverton						
Chiddingford						
Hurworth						
Alfriston (RNR)	(M1103)	Coastal Minesweeper	1953-60	153 (46.6)	28 (8.5)	29
Bickington	(M1109)					
Crichton	(M1124)					
Crofton (RNR)	(M1216)					
Cuxton	(M1125)					
Hodgeston (RNR)	(M1146)					
Laleston (RNR)	(M1158)					
Lewiston	(M1208)					
Pollington	(M1173)					
Shavington (RNR)	(M1180)					
Soberton	(M1200)					
Stubbington	(M1204)					
Upton (RNR)	(M1187)					
Walkerton	(M1188)					
Wotton	(M1195)					
Bildeston	(M1110)	Coastal Minehunter	1953-60	153 (46.6)	28 (8.5)	29
Bossington	(M1133)					
Brereton (RNR)	(M1113)					
Brinton	(M1114)					
Bronington	(M1115)					
Gavington	(M1140)					
Hubberston	(M1147)					
Iveston	(M1151)					
Kellington (RNR)	(M1154)					
Kedleston (RNR)	(M1153)					
Kirkliston	(M1157)	Coastal Mine-hunters	1953-60	153 (46.6)	28 (8.5)	38
Maxton	(M1165)					
Nurton	(M1166)					
Sheraton	(M1181)					
Wilton	(M1116) ·····(GRP construction)					
Abdiel	(N21)	Exercise Minelayer	1967	265 (80.8)	38.5 (11.7)	77
Aveley	(M2002)	Inshore Mine-sweepers (training)	To be replaced in 1982 by a new 23m class.			
Dittisham	(M2621)					
Flintham	(M2628)					
Thornham	(M2793)					
Woodlark	(M2780)					
St David (RNR)	(M07)	Mine-sweeping Trawlers	1972 1973	120.7 (36.6)	29.2 (8.9)	40
Venturer (RNR)	(M08)					

Name and Pendant Number		Class	When completed	Length	Overall dimensions Beam	Complement
Patrol Vessels						
Jersey	(P295)	Island (OPV Mk 1)	1976	195 (59.5)	36 (11)	39
Orkney	(P299)		1977			
Shetland	(P298)		1977			
Guernsey	(P297)		1977			
Lindisfarne	(P300)		1978			
Anglesea	(P278)		1979			
Alderney	(P277)		1979			
Leeds Castle	(P258)	Castle (OPV Mk 2)	1981	265 (81)		50
Dumbarton Castle						
Kingfisher	(P260)	Bird	1975-7	120 (36.5)	23 (7.0)	24
Cygnet	(P261)					
Petrel	(P262)					
Sandpiper	(P263)					
Droxford	(P3113)	Seaward Defence Boats (training)	1954	117.2 (35.8)	28.8 (8.8)	19
Dee	(P3104)		1953			
Alert	(A510)	Alert	1978	80 (24.1)	21 (6.4)	12
Vigilant	(382)					
Yarnton	(P1096)	Hong Kong Patrol Craft	1953-60	153 (46.6)	28 (8.5)	32
Beachampton	(P1007)					
Monkton	(P1055)					
Wasperton	(P1089)					
Wolverton	(P1093)					
Speedy	(P296)	Jetfoil	1979	90 (27.4)	30 (9.1)	18
Survey Ships						
Hecla	(A133)	Ocean Survey Ships	1966	260 (79.2)	49 (15)	115
Heclate	(A137)		1966			
Hydra	(A144)		1966			
Herald	(A138)		1974			
Beagle	(A319)	Coastal Survey Vessels	1968	190 (57.7)	37 (11.2)	39
Bulldog	(A317)					
Fox	(A320)					
Fawn	(A335)					
Echo	(A70)	Inshore Survey Craft	1958-9	106 (32.0)	22 (6.8)	19
Egeria	(A72)					
Enterprise	(A71)					
Ice Patrol Ship						
Endurance	(A171)		1968	305 (92.9)	46 (14)	124
Royal Yacht						
Britannia	(A00)		1954	412 (125.7)	55 (16.8)	270
Fast Target Boats						
★Scimitar	(P271)	Scimitar	1970	100 (30.5)	26.7 (8.2)	12
★Cutlass	(P274)					
★Sabre	(P275)					

2 Naval Air Squadrons

Aircraft Type	Squadron Number	Base	Aircraft Type	Squadron Number	Base
Sea Harrier	899	HQ Squadron, Yeovilton	Sea King HAS Mark 2/Mark 5	814	Culdrose
	800	Yeovilton/HMS *Hermes*		820	
	801	Yeovilton/HMS *Invincible*		824	
				826	
				706	

Aircraft Type	Squadron Number	Base	Aircraft Type	Squadron Number	Base
Sea King Mark 4	846	Yeovilton	Lynx	702	Yeovilton
Wessex HAS Mark 3	737	Portland	Gazelle	705	Culdrose
Wessex Mark 5	707		Wasp	703	Portland
	845	Yeovilton	Jetstream	750	Culdrose
	846				
	772	Portland			
	781	Lee-on-Solent			

3 The Royal Fleet Auxiliary

Name and Pendant Number		Class	When completed	Overall dimensions Length	Beam	Complement
Fleet Tankers						
Olwen	(A122)	Olwen	1965	648	84	94
Olmeda	(A124)			(197.5)	(25.6)	
Olna	(A123)					
Tidespring	(A75)	Tide	1963	583	71	110
*Tidepool	(A76)			(177.6)	(21.6)	
Green Rover	(A268)		1969			
Grey Rover	(A269)		1970			
Blue Rover	(A270)	Rover	1970	461	63	48
Gold Rover	(A271)		1974	(140.5)	(19)	
Black Rover	(A273)		1974			50
Support Tankers						
Brambleleaf	(A81)		1980	561	85	55
				(171)	(26)	
Pearleaf	(A77)		1960	568	72	55
				(173)	(22)	
Plumleaf	(A78)		1960	560	72	55
				(171)	(22)	
Appleleaf	(A79)		1979	560	85	60
				(171)	(26)	
Fleet Replenishment Ships						
Resource	(A480)	Regent	1967	640	77	123
Regent	(A486)			(195)	(23.5)	
Fort Grange	(A385)	Fort	1978	604	79	133
Fort Austin	(A386)		1979	(184)	(24)	
Stores Support Ships						
*Stromness	(A344)	Ness	1967	524	72	105
				(159.6)	(22)	
Logistic Landing Ships						
Sir Lancelot	(L3029)					
Sir Galahad	(L3005)					
Sir Geraint	(L3027)	LSL	1964-8	412	60	69
Sir Bedivere	(L3004)			(126)	(18.2)	
Sir Percivale	(L3036)					
Sir Tristram	(L3505)					
Helicopter Support Ship						
Engadine	(K08)		1967	424	58	73
				(129)	(17.7)	

Sources and Bibliography

The main sources for factual information in this book are official documents. The Directorate of Public Relations (Royal Navy) produces descriptive leaflets of all classes of ship, submarine and naval aircraft, and a valuable summary of the year's events in the Naval Broadsheet; the Director of Naval Recruting, as well as issuing a mass of material on career patterns and methods of entry, sponsors a helpful leaflet on *The Royal Navy: its Ships, Aircraft and Missiles;* the Royal Marines' magazine *Globe and Laurel* was a valuable source on the activities of that Corps; and the Statements on the Defence Estimates, 1980 and 1981 were essential for checking numerous facts.

Firms' leaflets proved a mine of unclassified information on weapon and sensor systems, and one of the best records of their introduction into service, as well as their history and characteristics, has been the *International Defence Review. The Journal of the Royal United Services Institute, Brassey's Yearbook,* and the publications of the *International Institute for Strategic Studies,* have provided valuable facts and opinions. Finally, the indispensable books of reference in the Jane's series are in a class of their own and no author on service subjects could fail to acknowledge a debt to them.

Chapter 1
Chatfield, Admiral of the Fleet Earl; *The Navy and Defence;* Heinemann, 1943.
Kemp, Peter (ed); *History of the Royal Navy;* Barker, 1969.
Lewis, Michael; *The Navy of Britain;* George Allen & Unwin, 1948.
Lloyd, Christopher; *The Navy and the Nation;* Cresset Press, 1954.
Marder, A. J.; *From the Dreadnought to Scapa Flow;* Oxford University Press, 1961.
Mordal, Jacques; *Twenty-five Centuries of Sea Warfare;* Abbey Library, 1959.
Parkes, Oscar; *British Battleships;* Seeley Service, 1970.
Popham, Hugh; *Into Wind;* Hamish Hamilton, 1969.
Roskill, S. W.; *The War at Sea;* HMSO, 1953.
Walder, David; *Nelson;* Hamish Hamilton, 1978.

Chapter 2
Berger, Rear-Admiral P. C. (now Vice-Admiral Sir Peter Berger); 'The Royal Navy: a Concept of Operations', lecture reported in the *RUSI Journal,* September 1974.
Cable, Sir James; *Gunboat Diplomacy;* Chatto and Windus, 1971.
Eberle, Admiral Sir James; 'Soviet Maritime Power' *RUSI Journal,* December 1980.
Gorshkov, Admiral of the Fleet of the Soviet Union S. G.; *The Sea Power of the State;* Pergamon Press, 1978.
Lewin, Rear-Admiral T. T. (Now Admiral of the Fleet Sir Terence Lewin); 'The Royal Navy in the Next Decade, lecture reported in the *RUSI Journal,* August 1968.
Martin L. W.; *The Sea in Modern Strategy;* Chatto and Windus, 1967.
O'Connell D. P.; *The influence of Law on Sea Power;* Manchester University Press, 1975.
Royal Navy Presentation Team Script, 1980-81.

Chapter 3
Garrett Richard; *Submarines;* Weidenfeld and Nicholson, 1977.
Garwin R. and Tsipis K., *In The Future of the Sea-Based Deterrent;* MIT Press, 1973.
Hezlet, Vice-Admiral Sir Arthur; *The Submarine and Sea Power;* Peter Davies, 1967.
Lipscomb Commander F. W.; *The British Submarine;* Conway Maritime Press, 1975.
McGeoch, Vice-Admiral Sir Ian; 'Changing Tactics beneath the Waves', *New Scientist,* 1971.
Ministry of Defence; *The Future UK Strategic Deterrent Force;* HMSO, 1980.
Sundaram, G. S.; 'ASW, the Key to Sea Control' in 13 *International Defence Review* No 3, 1980.
Whitestone, N. E.; *The Submarine – the Ultimate Weapon;* Davies-Poynter, 1973.

Chapter 4
Lyon, Hugh; *An Illustrated Guide to Modern Warships;* Salamander Books, 1980.
Preston, Antony; *Warships of the World;* Jane's, 1980.

Chapter 5
Milne, Lieutenant-Commander J. M.; *Flashing Blades over the Sea;* Maritime Books Limited, 1980.
Popham, Hugh; *Into Wind;* Hamish Hamilton, 1969.
Wragg, David; *Wings over the Sea;* David and Charles, 1979.

Chapter 6
Moulton, Major-General J. L.; *The Royal Marines;* Leo Cooper, 1972.

Chapter 7
Admiralty Manual of Hydrographic Surveying; HMSO, 1965.
Haslam, Rear-Admiral D. W.; Paper for the Nautical Institute's International Shipping Conference, February 1978.
International Defence Review, Special Edition No 12: Article on HMS *Brecon.*
Kimm, Captain P. R. D.; 'The Royal Naval Auxiliary Service', *Navy International,* August 1980.
Navy International; Article on 'The Protection of UK Fisheries', August 1980.

Chapter 8
Admiralty Manual of Seamanship; HMSO, 1967.
Sigwart, F. E.; *Royal Fleet Auxiliary;* Adlard Coles, 1969.

Chapter 9
Mason, Ursula Stuart; *History of the WRNS, 1917-1977;* Educational Explorers, 1977.

Chapter 10
Navy International: Article on 'Metamorphosis: Training in the RN', August 1980.

Index